Gauguin's Ghost Story

by Antony J Stowers

Contents

Special thanks to those whose hard work and knowledge along the road who helped make this happen – you know who you are. Front cover: the author.

1 – Gauguin's origins

The shaven-headed lunatic breaks from its chains and disappears across the rooftops. Servants with burning torches jab the air with sharp sticks and snarl orders at none who obey them, beating pewter plates with bamboo canes, spreading behind the rich houses and palaces, between the luxury and the filth, bawling and clattering to feel alive and brace against the unknown.

I watch them from my window high in the palace of Don Pio. I am a boy. I am a child. I am a dream only half-remembered. The scents of the flowers from the garden in the courtyard rise up, as do the speckled moths drunk on the beauty of the night, enticing my eyes to drown dizzily in the vast unending canopy of the deep blue sky, sticky with the white points of stars. I glance over and see on a low balcony, a woman's figure in a man's shirt tied loosely in a knot across her middle. She watches the hunt then turns and looks up directly at me, her brown arms leaning on the balcony, unfastened shirt falling open as she leans forward. She smiles, fans herself and turns away, pressing a cheroot cigar between her lips. Behind her the bright room fills with moving shadow and a swarthy naked man emerges and but for the concealing balcony rails could almost pass as a cloven-hoofed Centaur. His head tilts back as a pencil of wine falls into his gaping mouth from a calfskin bottle he holds above his head in one hand, the other encircling the woman's waist like a snake and she responds and they both laugh; a thin rope of wine pouring down his chin and chest like blood.

Far away a shrill scream cuts the dark of the night like a ribbon and a broken, half-naked figure on all fours scampers dustily across the dirt, its escape blocked by torchbearers until, trapped in a tight circle at their feet, it lifts its arms for mercy but the servants and downtrodden lash out viciously with sticks, fists and belts, thanking holy Jesus it's not them.

A soft Spanish voice calls my name and I return, curling beneath the huge white silk sheet with my sister Marie, the warm brown arms of our Negress servant fastening around us, humming a soothing lullaby as the cries of the lunatic outside fade to nothing.

* * *

I picked Stowers. He didn't pick me.

In January 2008 I was in Brittany, having gone there from Paris. In Paris I'd been with Vincent, traipsing The Louvre and ogling the beautiful girls but even that got boring after a while, so I'd caught a train out to Pont-Aven for the New Year. One advantage to being immortal is you don't have to pay for fares. For a start, I'm as light as a feather, much more agile than I was when I had a great bulk of weight to cart around on one gammy leg and I've squeezed into some amazing spaces since. Another advantage is I don't feel the cold. I don't feel the heat either, which is a shame because I used to love the Pacific heat, but there you go, you can't win 'em all.

Coming back to Pont-Aven in January was filled with memories, some great, some terrible. I was pissed off with what they'd done to my name and face: used it to sell everything from postcards to biscuits, tea towels to postcards and jam to beer. The town had grown a bit over the years, distorting some of my cerebral souvenirs but enough of the main arteries were still intact and brought a host of faces flooding back especially around the Lovers Wood and the church at Tremalo. I'd drifted down to the Hotel Julia in the mid-afternoon, except it wasn't the Hotel Julia anymore: where the guests used to sleep was occupied by the 2008 Town Council. The dining room below was still pretty much unchanged but had become an exhibition space. The ground floor, that used to be the cellar and kitchens, looked like a vacant meeting room. On exhibition were black and white photographs of the Hotel at least a century before. I had a glance and though I recognised no faces, it made me chuckle to think how if it hadn't been for the invention of photography, I may very well have stayed in the Stock Exchange, but in truth I didn't need photographs; I saw the room as I'd known it: a hundred people packed in, servants, trays and bowls of Breton cider, weaving crowds, tables fit to bursting, laughter, smoke, leaping flames, warming hands, drying boots, lighting clay pipes, back then . . . and there he was: Antony John Stowers.

I heard my name through that fog of a clumsy English accent explaining in bad French to the volunteer on the door he'd come to look at the possibility of performing a one-man theatre show about me and wanted to know how much this room cost to hire? I was intrigued. He didn't live locally - he lived in Angers. I'd heard of Angers, a few hours to the southwest, but never visited. He taught English and had been in France for two years. In England he'd made a little theatre as a writer, director and actor and had written a one-man show about me: Paul Gauguin.

I then had to seriously reconsider my future.

You see, part of the deal I made with Tioka in 1903 on Hiva Oa was I had to possess a new living body regularly and couldn't spend forever in the same one. He didn't say 'forever' obviously, he said 'eighteen moons' because it was more mystical but as it'd then been a few weeks since I'd abandoned my last artist, a Russian dancer, I felt it was time to move on. The Russian got some lucrative deals and furnished with sums disproportionate to what he produced started doing Class A's to cope. Hard drugs make spirits like me seasick - I'd seen enough with morphine and absinthe. So I abandoned him shortly before he OD'd and played stepping stones with a number of 'old meats', as I unkindly refer to non-artists, convenient hosts that enable me to get around. I tracked down Vincent and spent a few weeks in various bars but he hadn't changed: still argumentative and clingy, especially when drunk which was often. Then, in the ear of a fat American tourist, I hitched a lift to Pont-Aven where serendipity had entered in the shape of Stowers.

"I think you could use some help," he said.

"Ok, but don't fuck me about - amount of times I've been fucked about is enough to drive most men round the bend!" I barked back.

"The feeling's mutual", he agreed.

"Hop on!" he said and I did.

Once inside I got to know how much he knew. He hadn't done too badly: a small bookcase back in Angers held some good books and there was plenty in his memory banks. I soon realised Stowers couldn't get any closer until he understood more about Impressionism and he couldn't understand Impressionism until he knew what preceded Impressionism and what it was reacting against. He was reacting against something too but he hadn't yet seen the link.

I'd doubts that I'd made a wise choice – a glance into his memory banks revealed he'd had chances didn't seem to have capitalised, yet his back catalogue read well and his charm, blue-grey eyes and Viking jaw should have guaranteed him success, but there he was: mid 40's, almost broke, unknown, living in a rented box in Angers and driving a 15-year old car.

He also had a bad smoking habit, but who was I to lecture? I could have said twist but decided to stick. In total I've 'possessed' about fifty interesting artistic souls – male and female – in my career as a ghost, but multiply that by three or four and you've also got the failures I dumped. I suppose another deciding factor was getting to understand Stowers' journey and though he'd had opportunities to let ambitions go, he persevered because he felt he had something to say. I could relate to that.

So, let's just get stuck in: up until the middle of the 19th century, painting had become an art form shared by thousands but perfected by a few. The nature of art and artistic education is no different from other systems: success breeds success and eventually produces elitists who feel only they hold the keys to what's acceptable and unacceptable in learning, that is: what's important to learn and what isn't. So it is with art – some would say it still is - and so it was with art back then. In the mid-19th century art from central Europe spread out and influenced styles around the fringes of Europe and Japanese styles influenced Western artists and so on and for a long while painting was the only format available for recording our world, just as theatre was before cinema came along. Painting served as a direct mirror for the world and artists strove to reflect that reality in accuracy and colour as best they could. In this way, over the generations, a flat, representational way of thinking took hold and everybody thought and did the same thing, though their one big compromise was to understand perspective.

In France they created The Salon in Paris run by so-called Masters who deemed who was to have the chance of reflecting this accuracy successfully for the next generation and who wasn't and if your style didn't fit their thinking, you'd almost no chance and you'd not be able to sell your work. I hated them but needed them at the same time. Getting a painting into their annual exhibition got me noticed in '76 but that was about it. If anything it just made me realise I was a 'real' artist. Nobody had ever told me I was much good but when I saw strangers getting off on my work I realised all I really needed was a space and an audience that respected that space, not some old right-wing conservative berk telling people what was good for them or what wasn't.

When photography came along, untrained people suddenly had the ability to capture reality, in far greater black and white detail (and in much less time). Photography was an invention of science, unlike painting, connected through cave painting, horsehair brushes, oil-based paints and material-based canvasses, to the natural world and by the mid 19th century the effects of industrialisation were everywhere as machines interacted with human imagination and created a rapid expansion of materials and ideas. So the human race grew and, as it grew, so did it experiment and suddenly painters seemed to be out of a job. What use had the world for painters labouring away at canvasses, when a man with a box of slow-developing film could receive an upside-down image onto acetate and then transfer that image onto photographic paper in a specially designed room using chemicals and a stopwatch? And yet, the paradox was, everybody was free to express themselves, it didn't have to be all channelled through a small number of people who could control the output, shape it and cream off their ten per cent. The only exclusivity painting preserved by the late 1860's (photography had first begun to be used commercially in the mid 50's) was that to hire the services of a painter was considered a sign of affluence. Pass the sick bag. The Salon meanwhile stuck firmly to its traditions, as it simply didn't have the capacity to admit it could be wrong. If it did, its very existence would be under threat. Thus we see the true nature of the beast under pressure: it stubbornly sits there until forced to move or left behind.

So when a small handful of breakaway artists decided to throw caution to the winds and hold exhibitions of experimental work, it produced two reactions: one was the traditional world reeled about laughing and the other was that the commercial world, the world of the everyday onlooker, yawned, blinked and missed it.

Some of the principles behind Impressionism came about long before the term was coined. The idea wasn't dissimilar to those of, for example, punk rock in modern Britain in the mid 1970's, a genre I managed to learn about by picking Stowers' memories at night. God knows I heard his Sex Pistols and Buzzcocks a million times. Drove me fucking crackers but if it helps connect a few modern-day people who understand the importance of punk on contemporary culture get turned on to the deeper roots of new waves of thought through history, such as Impressionism, then why not? It's all action/reaction.

So, mid 19th century artists like Delacroix made ordinary people the subjects of his paintings, not rich lords and royalty who could afford the services of a painter. Ordinary people could identify with the subjects. Artists could open their minds to interpret what they saw and not what convention dictated they *ought* to be seeing and the audience had the choice to decide where to spend their money. It was Boudin who once told Claude Monet: "Three brushstrokes from Nature, influenced by the natural sunlight, are preferable and more alive than three days work at the easel in a dark room somewhere." Until then, convention dictated everything should be done indoors. The Impressionists reacted against that by doing the opposite and going *plein air* or 'outdoors'. I went a step further and, as well as painting plein air as the Impressionists did and the Englishman Constable had done before them, I combined what I remembered outdoors with what I painted indoors. For the Impressionists it wasn't that the whole world should see the same thing - for them the real value was what each one of them saw as individuals. What they painted was what the eye saw, the senses took in and sent out again in electronic impulses to the hand holding the brush. It basically meant that no two artists in the world could ever be the same and that was what was so exciting about the movement: it reinvented painting.

Theatre too is full of conventions and traditions and Stowers is proud to challenge those traditions as he attempts, in his own, infinitesimally tiny way to subvert norms and reinterpret forms. In 2004 he presented 'One of the Lads' in a Victorian school hall (a play about how he felt about the invasion of Iraq in 2003) and put the actors and the action in amongst the standing audience, trying to create a new but equally-grounded reality in each performance: "Remember: a thought process as you digest what's said to you, another as you prepare your response. Don't act!" It's not the reinvention of a particular art form - it's a reinvention of the self, how one thinks and feels and expresses as opposed to how one is programmed to think and feel and express. Maybe he wasn't doing anything unique or revolutionary but it was unique and revolutionary to him and his experience. It was Monet who inadvertently invented the term Impressionism: at one of the first exhibitions he'd titled one of his works 'Impression Sunrise' and a Parisian reviewer called Leroy leapt at it as a term under which he could easily label all those who dared to break with convention. But the Impressionists didn't see themselves as some sort of coherent group. They were all too individual for that. Only in style were there similarities: they used differing styles with slightly different uses of colour and subject and they didn't plan their paintings, aiming to achieve a fine finish of a serious subject and an exact replication of human vision. Instead they splashed colours on in spontaneous and daring ways in attempts to capture a fleeting moment of sunlight or a changing cloud. Their paintings appeared to the untrained as rough and ready and it was often impossible to see where the outline of one subject ended and the texture of another began. But by '86, Impressionist influence was on the wane. It was no longer seen as reacting against the Old. It'd been accepted and so almost immediately a New Wave evolved which in turn reacted against Impressionism – post-Impressionism. A whole new group of thinkers and painters were appearing, wanting to take what they'd learned from Impressionism and push into uncharted territories. This was where yours truly came into his own: Degas, Pissarro, Renoir, Seurat, Cezanne, and, finally, me were among this brave new band. It was Camille Pissarro who said our philosophy was an anti-authoritarian philosophy but that I personally was in error in moving away from it, but for my mind he should have kept his trap shut and just said: "Que sera, sera" because letting the next generation find for itself what it wants from an art form is the purest way to react to experimentation. The Old School, who'd first informed, educated and guided me, saw them as the Masters so I reacted against them then, with my own star in the ascendancy, younger artists looking for inspiration hitched on and eventually reacted against me. This is how it is. This is how it has always been. It's normal and it's healthy. But Pissarro and Cezanne became no better than those of the Salon: the old order telling the new order what was best for it is always a doomed stance.

I wasn't trained in any art school. I was untrained and self-taught. Some thought me opportunist, sensationalist, an upstart. Sure, I studied other works and spent hundreds of hours with other painters and questioned their theories and was constantly influenced by ideas but ultimately I never set foot in an art school. My style was very much a small portion of my own theory and snatches of the theories and practise of those around all mixed up and despite my prodigious output, I sold sparsely in my lifetime.

Born in Rouen in 1849, my parents had to flee France for political reasons, so they went to Peru to Spanish relatives. Unfortunately, my Dad died on the outward journey. Speaking mainly Peruvian Spanish, I spent the first 4-5 years of life there before returning to France with my Mam. I was enrolled in a Catholic school in Rouen and excelled in very little apart from art, which was rarely encouraged as a career prospect, in much the same way theatre art wasn't recognised as an academic subject in state secondary schools in England in the 1970's, as well T knew. In 1866 I signed up in the French Navy and spent the next six years sailing between Le Havre and Rio in what had to be one of the toughest career choices available: a stoker, not the wimp in gold braid pottering about on the bridge with the Captain mind you. I learned to sew, clean, cook, drink, fight and fuck – in that order and in 1870 I was on a cruiser that shelled Prussian positions at Calais, for all the good it did. In '72, with the war lost, I left and went back to Paris to discover my mother had died and our house had been wrecked after Prussian infantry had used the rooms as latrines. I was sad she was gone of course but with the death of both parents I had only myself to please.

By then a tough, burly and argumentative young chap, I was employed by Uncle Gustave as a debt collector and worked for a stockbroker in Paris, ensuring people who owed money paid their debts and it made me reasonably wealthy. I never had a lot of bother from people not paying up. Flushed with success, I met and married a Danish woman: Mette Gad. We lived in relative luxury in Paris, going on to have five children. She was a big lady, plenty to grab onto as they say, but I was naïve when it came to living in cultured society - I'd been living on a boat with 200 sailors for six years. I found cultured society fascinating and kind of fell in love with it all, as Mette Gad blindly fell in love with me.

In '82 I quit my job as I'd been doing pretty well with painting and thought I could take a year off and concentrate on it and if things didn't work out, I could always go back to finance. But it didn't work like that. I'd begun to dabble too seriously in what'd started out as a hobby. Influenced by the Impressionists, I'd spent a lot of spare time and money at the easel, my wife being happy so long as she lived in the style to which she'd become accustomed. I'd even had a piece of work accepted for The Salon in 1876, but it was widely held that it'd been accepted because it mimicked another style of painting known as The School of Barbizon. Bollocks it had – I just did what everybody else did: I looked at everything and then went away and made something that was mine. Nobody wanted to say "Well done!". It'd be like an Oxford Don telling an undergrad he was a genius – impossible.

Yes, it was a daft idea, looking back, the financial markets took a tumble and the marriage crumbled. True, I should have probably gone out and found another job but instead I clung onto painting as if it was an escape from reality and in a way it was. I tried Copenhagen with the wife and kids but fucking hated it – so conventional. I tried to organise an exhibition but was forcibly closed down so I split and went back to Paris with my son Clovis for a year, a bad idea - never had anything to eat and he was always ill and cold. The best I could get was a job as a billposter for five francs a day but I might as well have washed fucking dishes, like Stowers.

When things are bad the only way to forget how bad they are is to fuck your head up so I took up a lifelong interest in absinthe, a potent liqueur very popular at that time. Freed from responsibility, I turned my life wholesale over to painting and drinking. Being a billposter was one remedy but that was only about enough to sustain. Otherwise I hustled, lived from day-to-day and debt-to-debt as I learnt to play all and sundry and stay afloat, just enough to keep on painting and sometimes, but not very often, I sold some work.

I first went to Pont-Aven in Brittany in '86 and stayed for the summer as cheaply as I could to paint as much as possible and mix with other experimental artists who'd also gone there largely due to a sympathetic innkeeper called Madame Gloanec. Then I went to Panama and worked briefly on the canal before retiring to a broken down hut in Martinique with my friend Charlie Laval. Eaten to death by mosquitoes, I managed to get back to Paris with plenty of paintings but looking like a fucking skeleton and Charlie a year later as he was too ill to travel.

In '87 Van Gogh and I met at an exhibition in Paris and I realised straight off the guy had problems and in '88 returned to Pont-Aven where my work took on a new edge, especially with breakthrough paintings like 'The Vision After The Sermon'. 'The Vision' changed everything, everything. I got the idea from my mate Emile Bernard, I guess because I had a talent for developing and maximising the ideas of others - is that a legitimate job? I'll let you answer that. After I'd finished it, I didn't show it to anybody for days. I kept unwrapping and staring at it for hours thinking: "What the fuck is *that*, Paul?"

I did go to Arles and live briefly with Van Gogh. Bad move. Silly sod topped himself in '90. It terrified me that did. We'd talked about if often enough – if you had to do yourself in, how would you do it? I can't remember the answers. Soon after, I held an exhibition of my Panama and Brittany stuff to raise funds and in April '91, set sail for Tahiti, my main aim being to paint a world where I believed I'd find the primitive drowned by the West. And indeed I did, shagging, painting and drinking myself around, but no worse than anybody else. I eventually returned to Paris to shock the world but Paris was hardly shocked (few believed the foliage could really be as colourful and as translucent as I painted it) then an Uncle dutifully died and left me 9000F (about £900) and so I organised another exhibition.

I rented a studio in Paris, visited by artists like Munch - the use of lines around the central figure in 'The Scream' a direct result of my use of lines to emphasise movement I'll have you know - and the composers Delius, Maurice Ravel, Debussy and Greig, the playwright Strindberg and the sculptor Rodin and though they were still relatively young they all went on to become legends. Jesus, we had some blinders!

In 1894 I went to Pont-Aven for the last time and, in Concarneau, got beaten the crap out of, breaking my ankle in the process though I managed to lay two of them out. To make matters worse, I was diagnosed as having the clap and alcoholism. The alcoholism was no surprise - I could have told the doctor that - but I wish I hadn't shagged that last slag. Of course I'd escaped the precariousness of existence by drinking but I could hardly see any reason to stop drinking given that I'd been diagnosed with the clap. What is it better to die of?

Barely able to walk without a stick and numbed up to the eyeballs, I left for Tahiti in '95, never to return and tried to top myself in '97. Well, I knew where I was headed, you know? Better to get out while I was ahead: arsenic. But this stubborn constitution dictated otherwise. Eventually settled on a tiny island called Hiva Oa at what at that time was like the end of the fucking Earth, isolated at the end of a chain of volcanic islands called The Marquesas in the Pacific. I continued to paint (and annoy the locals) and it was there I died alone in May 1903, aged 54.

What the world doesn't know is the truth, about my death. And as long as the world doesn't know the truth, everything can be supposed. Shortly after his return to Angers in 2008, I planted a seed idea in Stowers' hypothalamus, watered it diligently and waited.

2 – Stowers' origins

Death's stalking me. It's stalking us all. A busy city street is like a fucking banquet for Death isn't it? Death must come in his pants when he sees a hundred thousand at a football match – a bunch of Reapers sat around the turnstiles playing cards. "Him with the cough – I bet you two matchsticks!" It's encroaching isn't it, Death? Like ivy, weeds or bad breath. It's constant stress, this life. Am I the only one to see that? Am I the only one who knows? I mean, I know that it's going to end but we're all encouraged not to think about it, not to talk about it. And the band played on. Knowing, it will but now knowing when my heart will stop beating - tonight, tomorrow? Knowing it will but not knowing when. I wasn't educated, that's my problem. I read too much trash. It's not my fault I'm like this. I'm an unknown writer on the dole. What did I do to deserve this?

At school I'd an eye for art and painting, even though my efforts were reduced to paintings of Jesus as he struggled up Calvary with a cross on his back getting beaten by callous Romans with hooked noses, or trying to carve a lump of wood into a human fist for a bedside lamp and the woodwork teacher scolding: "You can't do that – you're just a kid!" The rule of school is:

build up a store of knowledge supposed to serve you in good stead for the adult world, right? My time in school fucked me up. I recall my youth passing in a blur of dreaming. School, education, my teachers and the church – they were all boring, uninspiring and colourless. My only real escape was the world of books or I'd make up 'papers' for my family to read or hand-drawn books of cartoons for school friends.

At 12, I'd a run-in with the teacher that caused all these problems: Anthony 'Zeb' White. If it hadn't been for him I'd have been a working class lad with his house, car, garden and kid by now. Life would have been simple, right? I'd have been happy surely? Instead I got Zeb White as my English Teacher. Until this point there was nothing that separated me from anyone - half-kid, half-adult, nowhere, nobody, insignificant. His homework instructions were explicit: no more than 150 words in your essay. My first try got "When are you going to start writing with your real maturity and not like a child with a mental age of 5?" I was gob-smacked and challenged simultaneously and rose to the challenge and every week for the rest of that year got gradually better marks until I once scored 100% for writing an essay that asked "Is Mr White a Bogeyman?" questioning whether his strict reputation was merited. I was in seventh heaven, respected and listened to and all because of writing. It was his fault. He shouldn't have encouraged me. Threw himself under a train in the end. Why, because of what I wrote about him? I went to his funeral but they wouldn't let him be buried in a Catholic church.

"When are you going to get a proper job?" I want one but the voices don't. "What's your purpose on this planet? You know it has to end and there's a one in a hundred chance it's gonna happen peacefully in your sleep, so what're you scared of? When you gonna put Darlo on the map with your masterpiece?"

* * *

I don't know when it began. My Mam visited Paris on a school trip when she was a teenager way back in the 1950's and my working class life was so black and white as a kid that tales of my Mam in somewhere distant and exotic like Paris must have fuelled my imagination. It wasn't until secondary school that French as a subject was introduced. To many of my mates French was crap - what use did we as kids have for it in our everyday lives? Our world then was school, home, the shops and the playground. None of us would ever go to France, surely? We might as well have gone to the Moon.

We never visited France when I was a kid but went to Spain instead, who didn't? Escaping the confines of Northern England in 1973 (with strikes and shortages) to fly to a Majorcan town called Arenal where my until-that-moment grey and black patchwork world was blown to smithereens by the explosion of sunlight, colour and smells of Spain - tourism in its infancy. It must have cost my parents a whole year's work but what an experience: driving up to Newcastle Airport to board a real jet airplane and zoom into the sky across two countries and see the silver band of the legendary English Channel I'd only ever seen in a million war movies far below. Spain wasn't France but it changed my outlook, suggesting that the imagined world we'd only read about in books or saw on television really existed and that we *could* reach out and touch it even if we didn't come from rich families. Spain was the destination of choice for most of the North Eastern working class population in the 1970's, not it's geographically closer neighbour France, because of international airports like Newcastle and Teesside.

But references of France and the French filtered consciously and unconsciously into my childhood. My earliest memories are 1969, barely 25 years after the end of WW2, imitating 'Japs' (political correctness was unheard of) and Commandoes in the school playground. Us kids at that time, boys especially, were raised on a diet of jingoism and post-war Establishmentarianism, within-living-memory memory bells echoing to the sound of victory over the forces of evil represented by Nazi Germany, Japan and Fascist Italy. France played a prominent role in the jigsaw of our imaginations as we played soldiers, built Airfix fighter models, read war books and comics, collected photos of or bought monthly magazines that celebrated the legendary D-Day landings in Normandy in 1944 and opened out into A2 posters for a boy's bedroom wall. We were educated to the crushing horror of the First World War trenches in The Somme and then, stretching back, the final defeat of Napoleon. Beyond still further, films such as Henry V (with Laurence Olivier) or pictures of Joan of Arc and then 1066, a year most Englishmen mutter with bitterness.

In October 1981, two days after being fired for daydreaming from my apprenticeship as a printer in my hometown of Darlington in North East England, I arrived in Calais very early, just as a late autumn dawn was breaking, walked out to the edge of the ferry terminal and stuck out my thumb.

First I was taken to Paris and guided to the Porte d'Italie, an offshoot of the mighty traffic-carrying motorway called the Boulevard Périphérique that encircles the capital, negotiating the Metro and uttering my first clumsy words of French. It took a while to get a lift from there but luckily, as night fell on that first day, a driver took me through the night as far south as Lyon. After Lyon I made the mistake of accepting a lift that took me to a small town off the main route and I'll never forget walking through the deserted streets at 3 in the morning trying to figure out how to get back to the motorway I could see in the distance, wondering why I wasn't at home in Darlo tucked up in bed? Then a lorry driver took me as far south as Orange and I kept nodding off or spilling his scalding hot coffee as I battled against sleep but when the dawn came so did my renewed energy and it was about teatime I tipped up not too tired in Marseille. I could figure out where the sea was so turned a corner and knelt on the quayside, reached down and dipped the tips of my fingers below the surface, sparing a thought for the ex-colleagues who at that moment an hour behind were preparing to pack up work, switch off the hot-lead machine and lights, wash their filthy hands encrusted with ink and lead and think their own private thoughts as they moved in the empty space my unhappy presence had inhabited almost every day for over two years.

Then I panicked.

What the fuck was I doing in Marseille? It was as if the journey down had been an obsession, shielding me from important questions like: "What will you do when you get there? Where will you stay?" Two week's wages amounted to about 500F (£50), after the bus fare and ferry fare was taken care of and I'd only bought a one-way ticket. I pulled out my map bought in Dover to figure out the road route I'd need to get out of Marseille as I hadn't looked at it since leaving Paris and when I did and saw this mega distance between Calais and me and was suddenly gripped by panic.

Could I get a train back to Paris? It'd cost me all I had but it wouldn't be that difficult to get to Calais and from there to England and once in England nothing else mattered – I'd make it! But going back was chicken - I couldn't suddenly start crying: "Where's Mummy?"

I bumped into a guy dressed like a circus clown lost in Oxfam – he'd spied me standing by the side of the street and decided to cadge some cash. He spoke English so we struck up a conversation: Peter from West Germany, in the days when there was an East and a West, had skipped the military draft and fled to France, forced to live in relative penury for at least two years because if he returned he'd be forced into the Army. He calmed me down a lot that guy. We bought some bread, cheese and orange juice and shared the food as we sat and talked. I didn't have enough cash for even a cheap hostel so we bedded down on the hard concrete of an old warehouse down near the port. On my unrolled map he showed me an alternative route back to England, telling me he'd lived rough like this for a while by then and the first trick was not to panic.

Next day we were up early: Peter knew of a little port a few kilometres down the coast called Cassis. Bedding down there for a couple of days would be cleaner and safer than bedding down in a Marseille populated by muggers, pick-pockets and drug-addicts, the reputation Marseille had gained for itself through films such as 'French Connection 2' not being exaggerated. So we walked out, a day bright with the sunlight of Provence, to the edge of the city and picked up a lift to Cassis. It was an ideal place: a tiny little cove with waters lapping a pebble beach and one local food shop. We stayed two days and two nights, not really doing anything. It was hot enough in that October to still sunbathe and that's what we did and ate bread and cheese, drank orange juice, swam and ogled the few girls. But we couldn't stay forever and so he went back to his precarious life in Marseille and me further down the coast to see Cannes, St Tropez, Nice and Monte Carlo, places I'd been suckled on as playgrounds of the rich and famous through television programmes by the truck-full beamed into my working class home.

The plan was to leisurely wander down there stopping at these places but hitchhiking can rob you of the freedom to choose your destination. It's a necessity not a luxury. As driver of your own car you can stop where you like, but as a passenger in a stranger's car you've pretty much got to go where they're going and, if their ultimate destination is your ultimate destination, a smart hitchhiker knows it could be hours or days before another opportunity comes up to get to where you wanted to be in the first place.

My destination that day was Nice and Monaco, stopping at St Tropez and Cannes on the way but the car that stopped was bypassing St Tropez and Cannes direct for Nice, so to hell with Cannes and St Tropez, straight to Nice. I'd only wanted to go to St Tropez as I'd heard that's where rich women sunbathed nude and to a horny young teenager that sounded like a nice way to pass the time, despite having only lost my virginity in a one-night stand a month before to a girl, 5 years older than me, I met in a rock disco bar in Darlington.

"You've done this before haven't you?" she says.

"Sure babe, no problem!" I say.

30 press-ups in 10 seconds

"Is that it?" she says with disappointment.

None of the St Tropez and Cannes babes held their breath that day. The car, a yellow Citroen CV - an oval-shaped sardine can tipped on its side with wheels pinned on - had a canvas awning with a small rip in it and as we drove past cars from the other direction, turbulence filled the Citroen. So finally it had to happen - we passed a lorry and the entire roof filled like a balloon and ripped away, disappearing into the road behind and so we entered the outskirts of Nice towards evening in a CV convertible.

Nice was indeed the playground of the rich and famous but I was neither. After my staple diet of bread, cheese and orange juice, I wandered down to the harbour, found a small deserted rowing boat amongst the yachts of the millionaires, crept under the awning and unrolled my sleeping bag.

The only thing I was concerned with was getting safely back to England, but as each hour passed I could at least appreciate what little I could see and a glance at the map north of Nice was Italy's border and a little further after was Turin. My plan was Turin and hitch west back through the Alps into France - that way I'd get to see the mountain range I'd heard so much about but never seen.

I felt sorry for my ex-colleagues in their little ink-filled worlds selling their labour for money to pay their mortgages. Don't get me wrong - 30 years later I know it's an acceptable reality for most of the planet but back then it represented everything I reacted against and freedom, everything I loved.

The next day, under a clear blue sky, I hitched up to the Alps north of Nice, a variety of drivers taking me to the foothills then higher to a cold world of jagged granite, twisting roads, shadowy valleys, crystal waterfalls, sheer slopes, arched bridges and viaducts that spanned eternal drops. This was what I'd wanted to see and feel all those long hours in Darlington, staring out of the window as clouds scudded across the skies taunting me: "What are you waiting for?" Finally, I was at the top, a landscape of white snow and ice that spread out over most of middle Europe on all sides.

A single lift went from the border to Turin and I was dropped off in the middle of this dusty industrial city but felt disorientated. As long as I could preserve a sense of north, south, east and west in my head I could roughly figure which way was out but in Turin I just went to the train station and bought a single ticket for Susa, a small town on the border, as it was easier.

The journey took about two hours, with bread and cheese keeping me going. When I arrived in Susa it was night and very cold, I'd no money for a hotel and everything in my pocket was in French francs I'd bought in Dover. I was knackered, having walked, hitched and stayed awake since dawn in Nice so I unrolled my sleeping bag under the stars in the shadow of a hospital wall and slept like a lamb.

The next day was overcast and cold but I managed to get a lift from an old man with a white beard who was crossing to a town in France called St Jean-de-Maurienne. He was a sculptor by profession. He asked what I did for a living. I didn't know what to say. I think I wanted to say: "I'm a writer" but it was bullshit. I was nothing. I was a dreamer.

After St Jean-du-Maurienne, passing villages perched on stilts stuck into sheer rock faces, I got one exceptional lift all the way to Paris. I couldn't believe my luck and that night I was at the Gare du Nord, having bought a ticket for a train that left the following morning for Calais. I'd just enough to buy a ferry ticket back to England and then I was broke. Penniless and hungry, I bumped into another West German. Like me he was on his way to his home country the next day, so we teamed up for one night and roamed the streets around the railway station, begging and scraping together enough to sit in a warm, late-night coffee bar with two coffees that lasted an hour. When we put our begged francs on the bar we didn't have enough, so had to wait until the waiter disappeared before sneaking out. And he chased after us.

Next morning we parted company and I took my train to Calais. A jog to the ferry terminal managed to get me a single pedestrian ticket back to Dover and by that same evening I was back at a relative's home in London, tucking into a hearty meal after washing off the grime of my trek across France's roads. After toying with the idea of staying in London, I decided to get back to Darlo. I'd proved a big point. I'd done it. What had I done? I'd broken free.

"So," said my Dad "You've lost your apprenticeship and put the fear of God into your mother and me by running off to God knows where, so what are you going to do with yourself now?" "I'm going to be a writer and an actor," I said proudly.

They laughed for about a week. But I stuck it out and even ended up in drama school in the late 80's. It wasn't until 1994, in The Hawley Arms, a pub in Camden Town, London, I first met my French ex-girlfriend but now one of my best friends, Lulu. I was involved in a doomed enterprise when we first met, trying to sell ad-space and publish an international magazine paid for with advertising. A few months later my business went tits up and I high-tailed it back to Darlo. Lulu and I stayed in touch and I moved back to London in January 95 and worked in The Laurel Tree in Camden as a barman for about six months, fed up of the arsehole I'd become selling ad space. But there were just as many vices on offer in that bar as anywhere else in London.

In June that year we quit our jobs and drove down to France and for the first time I got to see a real French city – Angers (pronounced Onjay) that I wasn't just passing through and met 'real' French people. After, we drove to southern Spain and spent a few weeks living on a beach on the Atlantic side before driving back to Granada. It was outside the Alhambra Palace I decided it was time to go to Darlo to get my head together and life back on track. Lulu agreed to give it a try, neither of us were happy with where we were with our working lives in London. I'd actually nurtured the thought that one day I could always go back to writing. It didn't matter about making money, all that mattered was the ritual of sitting down with my typewriter and writing about my life or the world as I saw it but the only way to be able to do that was to find a less demanding lifestyle or go back on the dole and the only place in the world possible was Darlo.

So it was in September '95 Lulu and I tipped up in Darlo in an old Renault 2CV with some suitcases and two sleeping bags.

My French influences started with visits and visitors. Lulu had family in Angers, so she'd go back every summer and Christmas for the next four years. It was funny, interesting and challenging. We had our up's and down's in those early days, but nonetheless I had a gradual introduction to French, getting to grips with it and slowly learning to speak many years after stumbling across it at secondary school. Lulu and I split up in the summer of 2000 and she returned to Angers permanently but we'd both lived through her reinvention as a respected French teacher and me through my reincarnation as a playwright and actor from 1997 when I'd started writing plays for kids. She was in at least four of the shows I'd written. I spent a few weeks in Angers after we split up as we went through our amicable separation and then returned to the NE and shortly after started off a new life with Debby, a single Mum, and David, her son of 7, both of whom who had seen my play 'Cyrano' that toured the North East in 2000 and then 2001.

France was in my blood by then and within a year Debby had sold the house in Durham and we'd found a flat in the centre of Angers and stayed until August 2002, by which time the bubble of the dream had burst: we'd no work, were running out of money, Debby was struggling with the language and David was discovered to be dyslexic and needed urgent specialist attention in his native English. But after we returned to the NE, I missed my French life and one way to keep it close was to create Monsieur Gaston – French Shopkeeper, a character created to go into NE schools and help English kids learn basic French. I spoke enough by then to put together a convincing short show that proved very popular and gave me over 100 performances over the next two years. Another way I managed to keep my French connection strong was writing about Gauguin. In March 2003 as Britain and the USA invaded Iraq, Tony Stowers invaded Paul Gauguin.

3 – Gauguin on Stowers

"You're a Sunday painter, Mister Gauguin, but you're middle class. You're intelligent and educated and you rightly question the structure of society and its glaring contrasts. You can see the injustice, you can see the hypocrisy and it appals you but respectability is stronger than your desire to question the absurd discrepancies of the conventional. So you twirl your stick and toss it a coin if it holds out its hat and consider yourself sufficiently philanthropic but in reality you wear convention like a uniform. Your Uncle tells me you stoked the fires of ships for six years, down there in that inferno beneath the decks - don't tell me that when you had a break you sipped tea from China cups or recited Balzac? Now with your wife, children and house in St Cloud, suddenly you're respectable? Do you know what Manet said? Manet said: "No one is a painter unless he loves painting more than anything else." What do you think that means? Let me tell you: it means you must sacrifice. It means you must give more than you take. It means a life of uncertainty and a possible early departure from the stage. It means a life lived with no guarantees for old age. But you can't just swap your silks for canvas or your generosity for charity – the idea would be absurd. The change must be gradual

and what more gradual than becoming a full-time painter? Then you'll understand. Our little group doesn't criticise the true Masters, for to them we owe a great debt. We criticize only their servants, their shadows with their mediocre ways: the Greek figures, long-lost battle scenes and dying swans, rigid, formal and modelled on the Masters, copying the Masters but not making anything new. We don't paint the unseen, imagined glory of a world of Gods, mythical beasts or aristocratic nonentities garbed in armour. We follow in the tradition of Republican France: we paint the everyday world, not those with their fine clothes and carriages, perfumes and silk handkerchiefs. We fought a bloody revolution against such injustice. We paint soldiers and sailors, dancers and prostitutes, barrel-grinders and washerwomen, railway trains and factories - everyday people in everyday situations."

I turn away from old Pissarro and tune my ears to the others in the gallery.

"Infantile!" "Insanity, a child could have done better!" "Have you seen the music hall sketch, where the chap holds up an Impressionist painting upside-down and says you might as well see it that way than any other?" "They don't paint. Look, they

43

dab the brush on like children! And the subjects – where's the romance and the finery? Whores and beggars I can get for ten a penny outside."

"They're afraid of us, Mr Gauguin," whispers Pissarro. "They consider us subversive, revolutionary, downright dangerous. I know you exhibited at The Salon, but consider it as the Bible would consider the sinner: there's always time to repent. Like Jesus, you walk a dangerous road. As Jesus couldn't sell his politics, so we cannot sell our paintings and yet, like Jesus, we'd have it no other way, for to go back on all we've stood out for now would be a betrayal. Did you know Monet's favourite model died recently of hunger? Did you know I lost a child to malnutrition? I cannot clothe nor feed my remaining three. I send them to the coal yard to pick up loose coal that falls off the wagons and my wife spends much of her time repairing hand-me-down's and learning 50 Ways to Cook a Potato whilst bitterly demanding: "Why paint? Why not get a decent job?"

"Watch them," hisses Pissarro through his big grey beard.

"Listen to them. When it's all over, your life, nobody will thank you for it. If you know that early on and get the shock out of the way, then what do you have to lose?"

* * *

Memory banks are really just that when you're a spirit and inside somebody. You get to see everything. And, like a bank, it's a two-way process – I make deposits and withdrawals, depositing mild influences here and there - ideas that is. I can't operate arms and legs - I can only plant seeds or make some thoughts burn brighter than others. And I can refer to lots of other stuff that happened long before I came along, for consultation purposes.

I discovered some similarities: I'd been raised in a foreign country, spoke Spanish at the beginning and had to relearn French, forever afterwards speaking with a hint of an accent. Stowers had been born in England and had had to learn French, speaking forever afterwards with an English accent. I'd made money as a conventional member of society but turned a hobby into a full-time commitment. He'd dabbled in moneymaking for the sake of it and come a cropper with a failed publishing company. I'd never made a huge amount from my art but just enough to keep going and I'd believed in myself no matter who'd doubted. He hadn't made much from what he'd done either but that didn't mean it wasn't good work, it just meant marketing was in the domain of others. I'd left my native country never to return and died in poverty. Stowers was in poverty too but still alive.

What singles out greatness? All sorts of things I suppose but perhaps the most significant is *daring*. It wasn't just I was a bit flamboyant from time to time and it's not my compatriot was Van Gogh, nor was it because I lived and died in what's considered a Romantic era but simply – or so I like to think – 'cause I produced some good, original work and that work came about whilst all those around, for the most part, ignored me. We won't beg - we present our work and leave the decision to view it to the consciences of those concerned. Integrity's different things, a largely indefinable human quality that suggests those who keep their self-belief and their visions deserve it, so if my life means anything to me personally then it means that: for the subject matter, to be awkward, to react against any element that tries to control me and tell me my work is rubbish. To take control of the brushes in my hand and paint the colours onto the paper in any damned order I feel and fit them together in a manner that suits me – that's it, no more. *Yes*, we listen to others and *yes* we inherit historical traditions but ultimately imagination does the rest. It's the audience that decides, not the critics.

I was intrigued to learn I'd entered his head as early as 2003 – exactly one hundred years since I died. He'd spent about three weeks doing R & D with a variety of source material from Gateshead and then Newcastle libraries. He even went into Waterstone's bookshop and found some books about me but couldn't afford to buy them, so instead stood there pretending to skip pages but actually scribbling stuff down with a pencil. His final piece of R&D was to go The Laing Gallery in Newcastle to see the only one of my originals, a rather forlorn piece 'Breton Shepherdess' that looks as if it's been painted by a child with no imagination: dark colours, smudges and relatively unimpressive subject matter. Not my greatest work. That's only half the equation though – the onlooker or the audience has off days too but an audience isn't a group who behave identically, they don't all see and hear and feel the same. The weak audiences who like what they're told to like because their weakness puts them under the influence of educated individuals, they'll look around first to see what's being said before they themselves feel strong enough to join own opinion. I loathe them. Half the time they're not even aware they're doing it!

"I painted for love!" sounds like a fucking crazy thing to say but when I stop fighting my demons, that's what I see: love. I painted because I loved what I did and because I really did believe in some tiny way I'd give hope. Nobody ever forced me to paint but I felt compelled to contribute to this thing we call 'art', guiding us in some infinitesimal way towards human salvation. Between 1994 and 1997 Stowers continued to write theatre for children and over a few very short years racked up about 500 performances as an actor, with plays like 'Scars' based on his experience as a young vandal, 'My Brother Jake' about his London experiences, 'Colours' about racism, adults too with 'Cyrano' adapted from Rostand's great play and Steve Martin's 'Roxanne', 'One of the Lads' and 'X'.

In the late spring of 2003, he'd finished writing his 'Gauguin', a long and sprawling chronological history of my life from start to finish told through my own words and a myriad of characters I knew, rather than any storyline. So he scanned the world he lived in – Newcastle upon Tyne – and tried to figure out what to do with it. It'd be impossible to make with such a huge cast as he'd figured the best way forward was just to write it without regards to whether or not a large cast was feasible, that'd be a problem further down the line. All that mattered at that stage was to get all this wealth of factual information onto paper and into some sort of compacted form. The difficult part would come later, trying to find a way to trim it down into something to be presented.

His first attempt to start the story was to place it in a modern context at an auction where one of my works was sold for a vast and disproportionate sum, perverting the definition of 'value' but making me stinking rich. Then he tried kicking it off with me alone in my hut in Hiva Oa, in the final stages of syphilis, half-blind, barely able to walk, pushing pennies around on the bamboo floor singing: "What shall we do with a drunken sailor?" Next was where Anna the Javanese and yours truly were strolling along the promenade at Concarneau and got into a fight with the locals. I broke my ankle and when the pain hit I was rendered momentarily unconscious and slipped into a dream-state that opened a door to suggesting the surreal was possible as a story-telling device but it was a bit corny. The point was he didn't really know what to do with it. The circles he was moving in at that time - small-scale projects about drug abuse or language learning - were nothing on this scale and making enough money to pay for anything was beyond comprehension. His only regular expenses were petrol to get around (though often in other peoples' cars), food and, when he lived in England, tobacco and junk food. Apart from some schools work (performing for kids), he'd no regular income and what there was, was pitifully small.

Debby kept quiet about her thoughts but he knew it didn't bode well. Mette and I shared a similar situation. I suppose Stowers was hoping he might find a connected Director to say: "Well, this guy's done a good job so far, but now we need to help him", which is the sort of thing that might have happened had he had a company of his own or lived in a more sympathetic environment. But as a lone writer with no backup he was out on a limb and clutching at straws. He knew he *could* write. Why couldn't or *wouldn't* other people see that?

"Or is it true – am I really as crap as I think I am?"

Like Stowers I was out on a limb, in the wilderness, alone with self-belief and self-doubt. It was daunting. I managed to keep the terror of reality at bay through drink for years and would get depressed but my self-pity was more cathartic than productive.

I tried to be sympathetic, having been there, but if he wasn't feeling sorry for himself and thinking the world owed him a living and a few good reviews, he was out of his head dreaming about it.

He'd associated large ensemble pieces with the National Theatre in London so sent it there and it was returned by one of their readers with the notes that they liked the idea of 'the dreaming whilst unconscious just after passing out at Concarneau' bit but little else. After that, he stopped sending it out. There was no point in wasting money he couldn't spare in postage. Maybe the old rule still applied, even after years of experience: Do-it-yourself because most people are too busy trying to spot the next big thing to notice you.

In 2003 and 2004 he resurrected 'Space Jockey', a one-man show about selling advertising space, the first with a three-week run at Newcastle and the second with a month-long run in London. This was his second one-man show, beginning with 'London Cousins' in 1989. 'Space Jockey' was performed over three years in three different places, a re-write being needed after each performance, more re-writes during rehearsals and then cosmetic changes. It was first performed in Durham for three nights and Newcastle for 12 days over 3 weeks, one year later, and then 24 nights in London the year after that, so he must have actually read his lines close to 300 times. And even then it wasn't 100% perfect though this is the only foolproof method of getting a new show shipshape. His 'Gauguin' would be tackled in the same way.

By the autumn though I'd been forgotten and replaced by more pressing matters like putting food on the table, so Stowers figured if he ever moved to France he'd take it to Pont-Aven in Brittany in some way, shape or form and perform it. 'Gauguin' in its original form, did briefly see a revival in February 2005 when he managed to recruit 8 members of The Actors Centre North East to read the play. He called them the 'Cream cake workshops' because Gauguin was included with 4 other pieces of work he also read that month as part of a series organised through TACNE and featured so many actors he couldn't afford to pay them in any other form except cakes. This version featured two me's onstage at the same time, one examining and criticising the other with a series of "What if?" scenarios. It wasn't original at all but workshops aren't necessarily about originality, they're about experimentation.

Well, to cut a long story, Stowers struggled on in a marriage he couldn't save and it ended in divorce. By the summer of 2006 he was single and in July 2006 moved from Newcastle to Angers. Lucky for me he did or I'd not be writing this now.

4 – Stowers settles in

Look at these hands. Artist's hands, artist's fingers, slender. What these hands have touched. What have these hands touched? These hands have touched the softest skin. They've stroked and caressed the textures of the raw meat of steak, the cold, smooth bones of skeletons, the slippery scales of dead-eyed fish and the down on summer peaches. These hands have been burnt and frozen. They've gripped the handle of axes and hammers with tenderness and love and balanced brushes and pens with terrifying force. These fingers have pushed a lock of hair back from a beautiful face and held back a deadly thrust. Together they've rolled cigarettes, counted loose change, stirred coffee cups, added paste to a toothbrush, operated a million knives and forks, fastened belt buckles and shoelaces, untied ropes, manipulated keys in stubborn locks, pushed a hundred thousand buttons a hundred thousand times to change the view, made calls, opened doors, illuminated machines, typed a million keys, sent strangers to their doom or friends to their fate and they've unclipped bra straps and zips and cupped breasts and backsides. Curled into blocks of iron, these fingers have punched and hammered heads and doors. Talons extended, they've scratched and clawed faces, the sand, earth and the ocean. They've picked up pins and undone threads, extracted splinters and nostril hairs and run themselves through hair and fur. They've waved goodbye and shaken hands. Swollen with the pain of porting ten tons of metal or wood, they've been accidentally cut and sliced, banged in doors, bitten and stood on, scarred and blistered and then cleaned by the waters of a million baths, showers and sinks full of dirty soap. They've spoken with gestures, sending messages of love and messages of hate. They've scratched the body in every conceivable part it may itch, excavated snot and wax from ears and nose. They've held pens and tubes that have applied war paint to ugly faces, cradled babies and coffin lids, offered open palms in surrender and brought bodies to the brink of orgasm and into eternal sleep. Artist's hands work hard and if they don't work hard, they're not artist's hands.

* * *

It was a bright, sunny day, I remember that much.

I'd arrived in France the evening before, stepping out from the train with two suitcases after the connection from Lille where I had to change trains after the Eurostar from Waterloo. The night was warm with a scent flowers and coffee beans. With my two suitcases, I'd been met by an old friend who had driven me out to the countryside I knew so well, to his home – a detached arrangement of two small stone houses made into one sprawling bungalow. A few hundred metres away lay the banks of the gently flowing River Louet, a branch of the Loire River that flowed a few hundred metres to the north. Dragonflies the size of pencils flitted around the lamp and deep in the dark an owl hooted in baritone. Huge wasp-like creatures the French call *frelons* arrived to threaten and I then spent the night on a sofa bed being bitten to bits by tiny little mosquitoes whining in my ear as they inspected the *viande blanche* from cooler climes.

On the bright, sunny morning of that first full day, 12th July 2006, after copious amounts of thick black coffee, I borrowed a bicycle so I could go out and ride around the country lanes.

I'm a country boy. Born and raised in a small town, Darlington, always on the edge of (or never far from) the open countryside, wonderful scenery and landscapes throughout my childhood and youth, I'd gone with my parents to places like the Lake District, seaside towns such as Whitby and Scarborough and north to Holy Island, west to High Force, Teesdale and the Moors, south to the Cleveland Hills and Yorkshire Dales. In 1985 I'd gone off to Drama school in London and spent 3 years there and a further 8 running around like a headless chicken, working rubbish jobs, squatting, being homeless, getting arrested, scrimping and saving to get by, travelling millions of miles a year over the polluted capital, living my life, sacrificing quality for a struggle for identity and watching the manicured seasons passing in the London parks. After Drama School I had an agent and my future was being shaped but I was too young to know a good thing and I fucked it up by disappearing from London for weeks on end and so my agent let me go. After the safety of spending three years with the same group of actors and losing my agent and then losing my flat in Islington, I was suddenly in a vacuum and went wild for seven years, trying and failing to cope with maturity and allowing a potentially great career as a film actor slip by.

The trend has always been that if you want to be a famous actor you have to go to London but I was never very trendy. In my view people had to be mad to prefer pouring down an escalator on sweltering hot days in airless, black tunnels than walking along a country road under blue skies surely? But to make any kind of a successful career as an actor either in Britain or

France, the rule of thumb is you have to go there – Shakespeare did it - or Paris, but life in the city is the price to pay.

But you only get one life. I had to (and still do) ask myself: "Is that what you want? Or can you stomach living out in a place where that chance of financial success can probably never materialise, where only a small contribution can be made to the world through art, where talent will mostly go unrecognised and certainly unrewarded?" But surely art should be made in places where there is little?

Those first hot summer days brought out the snakes. I was unused to being in close contact with wild animals like that in Northern England, but in France they're common. On my bike I stopped and watched from a distance, fascinated as it slithered across the hot country road like a length of cassette tape in the breeze. Hawks too, bigger than anything in the UK, perched threateningly on telephone lines, like mini-eagles, launching themselves into the air, flapping to gain height, hovering on punishingly hot thermals before spotting some tiny prey and swooping down and I saw in the distance what I thought was a cloud of smoke hanging low over the road but when I got closer I shivered – it was a vast cloud of millions of bees droning their way slowly across the field, dust devils – mini-tornadoes – spiralling up into the sky.

I'd woken to a bright dawn far too early that first day, enthusiastic and eager, mind alive and active and wanting to investigate, wanting to make the most of it. I knew most of it well from previous visits but this time was different. Previous attempts to settle here had failed in 2000 and then again in 2002. In 2000 I'd been half-hearted about staying and had gone back to the UK to revive my play 'Cyrano'. In 2002, with Debby and David my stepson of 7 in tow, the three of us lived in Angers and managed to struggle by for 9 months without finding any significant income and returned to the UK defeated and despondent. But this time was different: this time I was single and recently divorced. I'd a small wedge of cash in my wallet and absolutely everything to fight for. If I didn't get my roots down this time I'd end up back in the UK and probably the North East dole offices again. Despite all my efforts to get some security as an artist, I might as well have stood outside Newcastle Central Station begging for change. Between 1997 and 2005 I'd managed to just about stay away from the dole office and live as an independent artist. It had brought a heady sense of achievement, freedom and self-respect, but untold stress – I never knew what the next day would bring – and there was no security, no pension, nothing for a rainy day, only the indefatigable belief that if I kept writing, one day . . .

I went to a local French café in the village of Denée that first day and drank far too many coffees because I wanted to just sit there and breathe it in and feast on the visuals of this small part of Anjou, an area so wild and beautiful it's listed as a UNESCO World Heritage site. By then it was midday and the sun was white and fuzzy and hot. I knew other friends nearby and set off to their home, struggling up a long, winding bank for half an hour or so, passing through a small village nestled in the short, rolling hills, host to a small part of the huge agricultural industry of Anjou in the form of crops, vines, fruits and cattle. Anjou is unique: an oasis protected by the Atlantic to the west, the rain that generally falls over Brittany to the north west and the warm wind and breezes that creep in from the south and south east. The giant thread that runs through all France is La Loire, a river that stretches almost 1000 km back into hills high above Marseille, over 30 smaller rivers feeding into it from all over. Around Anjou, La Loire's sandy banks spread out as the sea approaches, some 60 miles away just beyond the sprawling city of Nantes. Floodplains grow wider and more extensive and huge levees stretch along both sides to make the flatlands beyond habitable, keeping the potentially biblical flooding possibilities in check when 'She' swells in the winter and spring of every year, finally joining the sea near St. Nazaire.

Buildings near the rivers are often built on stone stilts with their electrical wiring sockets halfway up the wall or towards the ceiling to protect from the flooding. Insurers are conservative about homes built on these plains. But boats are everywhere, both as an attraction for tourists and fishermen and are a genuine means of transport and shuttling of cargoes. The capital of Anjou is Angers - a beautiful white city made of a building stone called tuffaut, the equivalent of chalk. From the centre of the city to the open countryside is only half an hour's walk. This region usually has such predictable weather patterns the majority of the entertainment is outdoors, courtesy of a spring that arrives like clockwork in March and retains a warm and encouraging breeze through to late October. The visit to my friend's house was incomplete without an *aperitif* so we'd chatted and drunk some red and then I'd left and freewheeled down the hill, intoxicated by alcohol and sunlight.

My immediate mission back then was to move to a house closer in Angers, on the outskirts. I stayed in Angers for a couple of months and began the more sobering business of finding a job that would get me a social security number and put together all I needed for a new life. I'd taken a book on how to conjugate my verbs but it was no best-seller, so the first thing I did was buy a copy of Stephen Clarke's 'A Year in the Merde' thinking I'd find comfort and learn some culture. At first I warmed to it as it gave me a few laughs but soon all the lines began: "One thing about the French is etcetera" or "French people are very etcetera, etcetera" which just seemed to me to be reinforcing stereotypes for the sake of laughs off a one-trick pony. But what Clarke experienced personally is one thing so I'm saying it now and won't have to say it again: this book does everything it can to avoid going down his path - if you're looking for stories of men in Breton jerseys carrying bunches of onions and saying "Sacre bleu!" forget it. I'd chosen Anjou for my home and Angers as my city and the people I met and worked with in and around the region weren't representative of an entire nation. Nor was I representative of the British.

Thanks to Lulu, I was soon installed on the edge of Angers in her house. I had a phone, a bicycle and a bed as well as an

Internet connection, a bath, a cooker and almost complete freedom to stretch my legs. It was a good start. But I needed a job.

In England prior to my trip I'd toyed with various ideas and made contact with a language school via the 'net, being invited to contact them. This was first on my itinerary. I cycled there on the second day in town, dismounting in a pouring sweat outside their building, my face red from the sun that'd stamped my white, pale Northern English skin with the word TOURIST. But I was far from wanting to be a tourist. I was here to stay. The school employed a recently pioneered method of teaching based on mild hypnosis - the use of repeated patterns set to music and song. We chatted for a while about how drama-inspired work might fit into their method but at that immediate time there was no work for me until September so I waited but promised to stay in touch. Although the timing wasn't great, with the summer holidays looming ahead at the end lay the possibility of agricultural work, picking either grapes or apples. It's tiring but I'd worked with Jews and Palestinians in Israel in 1988-89 on the Israeli *moshav* – a paid settlement of foreign volunteers - picking lavender, chrysanthemums, aubergines, melons and bananas. I'd been reassured by all French people *anybody* could find a job picking grapes (the *vendanges*) so it was a last resort. But beyond that, I didn't really know. I'd only vague ideas but an overwhelming sense of I mustn't fail or I'm going back to nothing.

In 1996-97 I'd studied TESOL part-time in Darlington and qualified as an English teacher but never had a chance to use it, as shortly after I'd written my first play for children 'Harry's Dream' and going into hundreds of primary schools and performing had taken over. A last-resort idea was simply to put together business cards and advertise myself as a private English teacher in Angers and had already written to the few language schools in Angers with a more detailed CV that covered my creative work in England but no replies were immediate. After a couple of weeks, the arrival honeymoon was over.

I went through a million doubts that August. In England, my colleague Zoe was working hard to put together a tour of Shopping with Shakespeare 2 (bringing short scenes of Shakespeare to everyday settings) and, despite the fact that I'd set up all the venues just prior to leaving England, it began to dawn on me that I'd probably not be able to get back in October and stay in France at the same time. Loving theatre and wanting so much to see Shakespeare happen in the diverse venues we'd found, such as a hospital, a high-security prison, a 13th century castle and half a dozen branch libraries but then realising I wouldn't be able to was a tough call. France won.

The first thing that hits you is the language. Everybody goes through it. How can a country so close to Britain geographically, be so alien in communication? 60% of English comes from French thanks to the invasion of 1066 but the pronunciations all got screwed up; in those days few could read or write. Communication was verbal so it was like a gigantic game of Chinese Whispers. The remainder is a mixture of Viking, Saxon, Roman and Ancient Briton and it's these guttural and flat stress-led sounds that batter the dancing tongue of syllable-led French into sounds we recognise as English. Look at French words and you can see their roots in the English vocabulary but it's the *sound* of French, through the language, that really threw me. Meanwhile, as the hunt for a job went on, I'd found a local supermarket and, mostly by looking at pictures on the packaging, managed to stock the fridge and freezer of my new home, situated as it was on the border between Angers and its smaller neighbour Trélaze but the trip into the centre of Angers could only be done by bus, as it was at least 3km. I cycled it a couple of times but in July heat it was a belter.

I found the then-French equivalent of the British Job Centre – ANPE and registered (with my broken French and unconjugated verbs) and then turned to the PC's that lined the room. Surfing for a job is how it's done in France. I wasn't claiming any dole as not only could I not deal with in-depth conversations but, as I hadn't worked at least 900 hours the previous twelve months, I'd not get any anyway. I was amused to discover how claimants could sign on over the Internet and at any time within a recognised period at the end or start of every month, no strictly enforced signing-on times as used in the UK. At my first interview I managed to explain how I'd like to sell myself as an English-Language Drama Teacher to schools and businesses alike and how did I go about registering self-employed and so was directed to the Chamber of Commerce in Angers, AKA palmed off.

I remember the Chamber of Commerce from my previous stay five years before - Debby and I had gone to dinner with one of their English reps to explore using theatre as a tool to improve working practise in companies, but the rep had politely told us he felt that Angers really wasn't ready for such a radical approach. Five years later, further enquiries led me to another building where a lady showed me on her computer how my trade, known as 'Creative theatre artist' in Britain as was my choice, is in France known as an 'intello' which means 'intellectual. I burst out laughing – nobody had ever called me one of those before. There were also heaps of employment agencies but what could I do? I'd trained as an actor and wasn't famous, not that there were any jobs for me in a little city like Angers anyway. I had no manual skill other than my muscle-power or my teaching qualification.

Regardless, I patiently photocopied my creative CV 30 times and bought envelopes and stamps, sending letters out to primary schools and colleges seeking to work with students and teachers wishing to use an English-language-based drama artist to teach English. Only one reply: a college. I borrowed a car for the day and drove up and had two positive meetings with French English and Drama teachers, showing them examples of my work in England. They were keen to employ me as a Drama Teacher who worked in English but the problem was my status.

Who did I work for? Good question. No status – no job.

I went home and switched on the French computer to find out what my status would be and the screen came to life - in French. Luckily all the boxes were in the same place for Windows as they were in English, so I managed to find my way around by the familiarity of the patterns, but the keyboard remained infuriatingly unfamiliar to my typing fingers, the top line from left to right being AZERTY not QWERTY. I put together a CV that made it look as if I'd been a manual worker all my life in order to get any kind of work I could in Angers, just to get my foot in the door: funeral parlour, barman, dishwasher, driving handicapped kids to school, bus driver, chicken farmer. Unfortunately, the consumer revolution has yet to hit France – CV's and qualifications are still far more important here than personality, a smile or willingness to try. In the UK we look for potential, in France they look for achievement.

As all this was going on I saw an article in a local newspaper about an organisation that received old and used Mobilettes (mopeds), renovated them and then hired them out for next-to-nothing. So I went down next day – and it was closed. It was after all, half past midday! The staff rotation concept is growing here but often if one goes to lunch, generally all go to lunch and office or shops are closed, no quick affair, in many cases at least an hour and a half. In France the client or customer is not the king. La Poste (the French equivalent of the Royal Mail) seem to think customers ought to be grateful they exist at all. I've been hear three years now and it still frustrates me that I can't get what I need when I need it nor do shops and public utilities buildings seem to be laid out properly.

The 35-hour week seems like a proletarian dream come true but there are disadvantages. Teachers, for example, can only work Monday, Tuesday, Thursday, Friday and Saturday mornings which means students too are forced to shift their lives around this timetable, as are parents. Of the 52 weeks in a French year, 16 are school holidays and 11 public one-day holidays. Banks are closed on Monday (but open Saturday) and given that France has twice as many public holidays or saints days as the UK, this often means the French will create what they call 'un pont' (a bridge) by connecting a weekend with a Tuesday or a Thursday if a public holiday falls on a Tuesday or a Thursday. So they'll take off the Friday or the Monday as well and nothing moves from Thursday until Wednesday. The French seem to work longer hours per day but fewer days per month. So it's a country of paradoxes, but then so is England, so is America, so is any country. We all have our idiosyncrasies. France is a complicated place, made up of strong sections of socialists, conservatives, nationalists and communists, but then isn't that democracy in action?

Pro-British and American cultural iconic touchstones in cinema, theatre, rock and roll mean much less in France. It really is a back-to-the-drawing board type of challenge, having to relearn how to communicate and re-educate oneself to what cultural and political touchstones are important and whereas Britain is heavily influenced by Asian and American cultures, France is heavily influenced by African cultures and Molière is the French Shakespeare, though nowhere near as prolific.

So I managed to figure out (after eventually managing to find the Moped Hire factory open) the costs of daily hire and within two days paid a deposit and was sitting on a 50cc Moped, looking every inch like a monkey on the end of a stick with my full-face visor. I managed to work out I wasn't allowed to take the moped more than 25 km from Angers in any direction. With the aid of the map I was able to draw that radius around and limit my job search. I also discovered (to my shame) that my moped didn't like anything that resembled a hill – the engine would simply give up and roll to a standstill, or the spark plugs dropped out occasionally when I stopped at lights. Do you have any idea how ridiculous you feel *pedalling* a moped? I was like a clown at the fucking circus! Thank God for the full-face visor to hide my shame! But getting a car was impossible just then and though a moped looked stupid and I looked twice as stupid, it meant I could get around town and be able to get to job interviews - if I could get any.

Rather than trying to get jobs I knew or had done before, I tried for everything but it's funny getting past 40: in my head I still felt young and active but the lines, wrinkles and grey hair belied the fact that I was no spring chicken, so try as I might to get a job as a barman in a club for young people, it still smarted to be turned down, which is what happened when I occasionally cut the corner by going straight to the bar or restaurant that was looking for a barman, rather than send off a letter. What I lacked in communication skills, I made up for in enthusiasm but it made no difference – I was an old foreigner! I didn't have a chance of getting a bar job - I couldn't communicate even simple things like numbers, but I kept on trying, believing something just had to give as the two grand I'd brought with me wasn't going to last forever. I found myself a bank (Credit Agricole, I liked the name) so I could regulate withdrawals and spending better with a *Carte Bleu* credit card. Then I bought a mobile phone - and it took a return trip to the shop to learn how to switch it on as the instructions were in French. My *Carte Bleu* could be used like a credit card in supermarkets and shops but never having had much cash in my life I was paranoid about losing track. In the UK we have credit cards of course but they simply weren't as common or used as widely and as often as in France. Still, with a mobile, a moped and a bank account I was reasonably well armed to do battle with the modern French world.

5 – Stowers on Gauguin

Tahiti: a paradise and yet I'm a tourist. I feel secure, as a tourist, one who can dip into the pool leisurely with the certain knowledge that I can leave anytime I want. I'm a visitor. I want to feel a part of all this and yet I stand out with my white skin and clumsy-boned lumbering crate of arms and legs. Every day the villagers wake and float about in brightly coloured sarongs like so many flowers under a canopy of the bluest blue that blue can be. We eat fruit and fish in groups scattered around on the sand under the palms where a constantly warm breeze plays around us, floating across from the distant breakers and the coral reefs.

I spend hours looking out to sea, wondering why I can't be part of it. And now I realise why: I miss you. I miss those things that made me feel whole: love, marriage and you, my tongue-tied magnificent Dane! How I wish you were here by my side, the two of us like children again as we were all those years ago in rue Bolard in Montparnasse, our children around our feet. And yet, even then it was an illusion of sorts. You knew that. I knew you knew that. We were so different – all we had in common were the fine clothes we wore – we were both suffocated in the respectability of it all. You must have known, must have suspected? The alarm bells rang for you as they rang for me and yet we were under the spell. Like drunken youths, we welcomed it into our lives.

How I worshipped you, your body, those full breasts of yours that fine rounded back, how I loved to pull you onto me and drown in your flesh before burying myself. I promised you this paradise and I've delivered but I know now you're a ghost to me and like a ghost, your imagined voice and our imagined joy haunt me. You're in me, my love, until the day I die. You speak to me and guide me. You're the spirit of my Tahitian vahine. I thought for so long I was a beast of the field, feeding and rutting but I'm not am I? I'm a civilized European playing the role of the primitive. And so, the search for you guided me to a village called Faone. I tethered my horse outside and the villagers invited me to eat with them. They know me here not as a painter but as "the man who makes men". A woman around my age asked me: "Where you go?"

Tell her, I heard your voice say to me

"To Itia," I said, "To find a vahine."

"If you want - is many here, good-looking too. Yes? This Tehura - she from Tonga."

Tall and strong with big breasts and golden-brown skin, she moves gracefully. Her dark hair, parted in the centre, falls over one shoulder. Her forehead is broad and high, her eyebrows thick, black and straight, her eyes dark. She's so young and yet so sure of herself when she looks into mine. I'm entranced, hypnotized. I feel that surge within – lust stirred with love, that same feeling you and I shared so many years ago. She isn't you but I know you're in her. I see you behind her eyes when she looks at me. I didn't know what to say or do. Imagine – me, lost for words! I thanked them and mounted my horse and as I began to ride back to Mataïea where I live, I noticed Tehura walking behind me some distance and behind her a little further her family following. Ahead of me was a hut by the road and a woman stood outside as if waiting for me. No words were spoken but I dismounted and followed her inside once her arm had extended an invitation. Tehura joined us.

"Are you a good man?" asked the older woman, stepmother of Tehura.

What a question.

Last night I visited Papeete and had to walk home very late. My hut was in darkness and so I struck a match and pushed open the door. There she was - lying on the bed face down, naked, her frightened brown face and those big doleful eyes. She was terrified, like a child, of the 'tupapaus' - the evil spirits she and her people are convinced inhabit the forest at night. She snuggled into my arms for safety. I closed my eyes and saw you, felt you beneath me and I exploded in golden light. I told her I loved her and today I paint 'Manao Tupapau' which means 'The Spirit of the Dead Is Watching'.

* * *

As Anjou is largely dependent on agriculture, there are always plenty of jobs on farms or in greenhouses. It's hard work but I'd done it in Israel 20 years ago so knew I could do it and through visits to ANPE (the French unemployment office, Labour Exchange or Welfare Office, today re-named Pôle-Emploi) I figured out the address of an apple farmer in a village called Ecouflant on the edge of Angers and went up on my moped to find his farmhouse surrounded by fields of apple trees laden with apples and camouflage netting. In those first weeks I was intensely conscious of my accent punching its way out on every syllable and struggled with basic greetings, employing French words but giving them an English structure to match the thoughts in my head. I approached the farm and saw a tall, thin man and asked if he was Mr So-and-so and received a curious look, so then I asked him for him by his Christian name Denis (pronounced as in the legendary pop song by Blondie). I'd pronounced it like the cartoon character in the Beano. Talk about a withering look! After all, he was the wealthy landowner and I was the lowly apple-picking labouring scum. Nonetheless, he promised I could start for a one-day trial at the end of August and if it went well I'd have 5-6 weeks paid work at the SMIC rate, the French name for the minimum wage.

" 'ave you picked apples before?"

Last time I'd picked apples I'd been about 12 years old and stolen them from an allotment and I didn't even eat them - just used them to smash windows. Denis and I lasted one whole day. Along with other workers, we passed along rows of trees and instructed to pick apples that were more red than green. At the end he brought me into his office and said: "I don't want you to come back – a 12 year old boy knows ze difference between a red apple and a green apple." I struggled to form in French the words: "You can take your apples and shove them up your asshole!" but didn't – try to say something you think is an insult in French and get it wrong and it backfires totally and *you* end up sounding like the asshole. There were too many of us and he had an excuse to lighten the workforce. Voila.

So I had to keep looking, hard at times though to get motivated as summer was in full swing and the tourist industry wide open, bars and terraced cafes spilling out into balmy streets and evening temperatures of 90F. Temptations to relax and spend cash were everywhere.

I'd been to a French friend's party a few days after my 43rd birthday and met somebody who said they lived in a vineyard belonging to a local chateau and were sure I could find a job, though everybody told me the *vendanges* wasn't likely to be starting until the end of September as, officially, the French government decides the grape-picking date. So a few days later I'd gone on my moped down to her home near the village of Rochefort, south west of Angers. It was the absolute limit my moped was allowed to go and it conked out going up the steep but short hill through the vineyards where, nestled amongst two other houses renovated and converted from what was once a working windmill, now absent of sails, was her home. Later on, together my new friend and I sauntered across to the chateau. Having found Luke the *viticulteur* and given my name and address, I was told I'd be contacted in September to start for a three-day trial period. Way-hey! I had a job! I'd never picked grapes before but felt that whatever else I did in my life, the journey wouldn't be complete until I had. And I needed the money.

Meanwhile, I was running out of time, the friend who'd lent me her house was due back and we'd have to adjust to one another's presence, a gamble not guaranteed to pay off. Although I had a job offer, it didn't offer a regular wage or security just a temporary cash injection. There are two forms of working 'contract' in France: the CDD (contrat durée determinée) and the CDI. Almost everyone has one or the other. A CDI (contrat durée indeterminée) is a contract without a pre-determined end. Apple or grape-picking jobs are CDD's (contrait durée determinée) because you can't pick apples forever. CDI's often have lower wages than CDD's, but not always. The argument is that the wage can be slightly lower because job security is guaranteed whereas the CDD is a short but often-profitable injection of cash for a limited period.

Anyway, around the 20th August I bumped into an old friend in town, a teacher called Pierre. We hadn't seen each other since my last stay there in 2002. When discussing my problems looking for a job, he suggested I went to the City Administrative (Local Government Offices) and asked if they needed English Teachers or English-speaking assistants for their primary schools.

Genuinely English, English Teachers are far and few between in French schools, the vast majority French-born. What Maine-et-Loire Education Authority do is recruit about 30 young and inexperienced "assistants" from around the English-speaking world to be paid to live in Angers or its satellite towns for 9 month contracts to work about 12 hours a week 'assisting' the official French English Teachers. Well, no sooner had I walked in the door than the lady responsible looked at me and said: "It's Tony Stowers! How are you?" I had no memory whatsoever. She had to remind me: four years previously I'd toured an English-language show called 'Talk To Me' to four primary schools in Angers and she'd been Head Teacher of one. Four years later she was responsible for promoting foreign language throughout the county and she offered me a job there and then but because my French wasn't 100% I didn't quite believe it, it seemed too easy to be true and it took my friend to phone City Administrative to establish the truth: I had been offered a job as an assistant English Teacher, working with a French English teacher in three schools in and around Angers. I had another job, with a better wage and a profession more suited to my skills. Relief!

Meanwhile, I started picking grapes near Rochefort-sur-Loire. The romance of the situation dissipated in about three hours. Rain or shine (and both were punishing), we were expected to be out either stripped down to t-shirts or covered up with oilskin coats, holding lethal *secateurs*, fumbling through the dense branches of the vines with one hand holding onto to the bunch of grapes to separate out the stem and then cut. Accidents were frequent for all of the 12-strong team (of both sexes and various ages) for the first week and we finished each day caked with a mixture of sweat, dried grape juice and blood.

Different types of grapes produce different types of wine and these different grapes grow on different types of vines: some waist-high, others on vines that sprawl out of the ground, others shoulder-high. Standard plastic buckets are filled and then they shout *"Seau!"* (French for bucket) and all the pickers stop at the same time and pass their full buckets under or over the wires that fence off each row of vines. The person closest to the *benne* (the deep trailer pulled by the tractor down the central row) empties all buckets into it and passes them back again. I was given this job along with another big guy on the other side, but lifting heavy buckets one minute and then breaking your back bending over to pick grapes from ground-level all day long is no easy feat. We'd been equipped with long green waterproof jackets and Wellies when it rained. I thought we'd simply stop working until it stopped but I was told the combination of rain and light increased the yield of the grapes (I'd never heard such a thing but these people must know what they're talking about). Some mornings we'd start work in fog so thick we couldn't see more than a few meters ahead and within minutes a burning sun would be blazing. We'd see animal droppings and be warned to look for *sangliers* - boars. Boars still roam wild in many parts of France and though I've yet to see one in the wild, I remember hearing them one dark night rutting in the darkness of the vines with grunting noises like pigs. I've always been told not to be brave if stumbling across a boar but to run as fast as possible.

No problem. They're the favourite game of hunters and there are plenty of hunters in France, mostly frustrated civil servants, office workers or computer programmers by day who dress up as Rambo and go around in groups blasting away at anything that moves on Sunday hunting trips, occasionally each other.

Nathalie, the team manager, gave us a pause around 10 and 3.30 for hot coffee from a flask and slices of cake and we'd have an hour and a half for lunch back at the canteen near the chateau. The trailer loads of picked grapes were put into a hydraulic vacuum barrel and hundreds of gallons of wine juice squeezed out into large vats, treated with sugar to bring out the alcohol and left to ferment for 12 months. The chateau had three such tanks each holding 30,000 litres.

The majority of French vineyards still use hand-pickers to harvest their grapes but an increasing number use harvesting machines operated by one man which straddle the rows of vines, beat the bushes to break the stems and then suck everything up into a container. The problem is that *everything* is sucked up and after the 'machine' as the refer to it like a kind of cruel beast has been through a field there's nothing left at all, no wildlife, no insects, not even boar droppings. We saw our fair share of accidents – chatting away to break the boredom of rustling and fumbling around in dense undergrowth looking for a 1 cm thick stem to snip with sharp secateurs. The season lasted four weeks for me and didn't finish with a bang but more of a whimper: the gang master announcing, in mid-morning and at the end of an old row of grapes "C'est terminé!" Well, I'd done it – I'd cut grapes and got paid about 1000€ for five weeks. It wasn't a fortune but it was the first significant lump of money I'd made in France since arriving and wouldn't be the last.

I began working as an Assistant English Teacher. After attending a preliminary three-day introductory course to educate myself and 25 other English-speaking assistants from around the world, I was given start times and two local primary schools and began working with Veronica, my French English Teaching colleague. I worked only Tuesdays and Fridays, meeting up at the first school and taking two classes, then getting in my car (I was driving my French girlfriend's Peugeot 205 by then, left hand steering, right hand side of the road) and driving to the next school, doing two consecutive classes and then, after lunch, taking two more classes in another school. My contract was only 9 months long and guaranteed about 800€ a month but it wasn't so much the amount that appealed or the hours - it was the security: I could relax and find my feet.

My teaching role was limited and I learned quickly that an assistant is just that: assisting in teaching methods already devised. I didn't like them very much (the teaching methods) but shut my mouth and did as I was told because this was the best chance I'd had to get some roots. My job consisted mostly of drifting from table to table ensuring the pupils got on with what they'd been instructed. My colleague spent at least 5 minutes of all 50-minute classes focussing purely on discipline. I thought it was crazy to waste such valuable time trying to get kids aged between 7 and 10 to fold their hands and sit in silence like little robots and favoured relinquishing some of that control by doing away with tables and chairs and making open spaces and so whenever I got the chance I played games where kids had to get up and mime certain sports or actions and others had to guess in English what they were doing. That was a far more useful and constructive way of harnessing energy than trying to control it. But I walked a fine line – I couldn't let it be seen I appeared too imaginative and I didn't want to fuck everything up by losing my job and ending up back in Gateshead.

Nonetheless, the head of foreign languages called me into her office a few weeks later and I thought I was going to get into trouble, but she outlined a special project she was running just before Christmas and asked if I'd be interested? It wasn't extra cash but I'd be taken out of school for a week and spend five days working at a special unit on the outskirts of town in a renovated building kitted out with beds, a kitchen, playrooms, canteen, computer rooms, a park and so on – an extended-stay centre for kids from poor or under-privileged backgrounds.

I was given two groups and got to work with them at staggered periods throughout the five days, the theme of the week being 'Speaking English'. Other activities were organised with other teachers – all French of course – and the event filmed.

Once I'd completely understood what they wanted me to provide over the course of five days, we worked towards a goal, i.e. something that could be presented to the parents at the end of the week, giving a sense of focus to the five days. I used many of the games and TIE shows I'd played over the years, adapted to get the kids to speak one or two words in English and then to increase their 'Christmas vocabulary', as well as learn how to construct and speak simple sentences. There's some film of me somewhere leaping and jumping about. One group was more adept at meeting the demands than the other, but that didn't mean one group was clever and one group wasn't, it just meant that each had different skills. Group A got to work on the song 'The Twelve Days of Christmas' and Group B got to learn the English necessary to instruct their parents how to play Christmas Bingo. The prize for the Bingo we coaxed out of the Centre was a free meal, courtesy of the chefs. My Mam sent over the CD she'd found in an English record shop featuring crooners singing classic Christmas songs. I had Bing Crosby's classic and managed to get the kids familiar with the tune, then taped up long lengths of white wallpaper behind me and across it wrote all the lyrics in big letters. It was here, with my back to the wall and the kids in front able to look up at the lyrics and me, we rehearsed together. The other Group made up cards with pictures of traditional Christmas images - snowflakes, skis, holly, Santa on his sleigh etc - and learned the vocabulary necessary for placing cards over the images once the item was called by the kids themselves lifting the cards out of a bag.

Not all the parents turned up at the end of the week, it was tough having to try to cheer up kids whose parents (alcoholics or drug addicts) didn't give care to turn up, crying their little eyes out, but the Bingo event out of the way, we finished off with a well-rehearsed and stirring rendition of 'The Seven Days of Christmas' rather than all twelve, having weaned them off the words so they were now singing purely from memory and practise. I was proud of them all.

In January 2007 I drove back to Darlington to pick up my computer and some personal belongings and returned again to Angers to restart work with the schools. A month later I'd another call from the Education Authority asking me if I'd do the same thing with another primary school visiting the Learning Centre. The approach was slightly different. The teacher of the school already had a clear picture in his mind of what he wanted. When I understood, I wasn't keen at all: the teacher favoured a traditional classroom-based approach and wanted me to stick to his plans for the week. The urge to want to take over and dictate the order of play was strong but I'd been invited to support and not be a co-partner and that meant letting the teacher have the final say on everything and me offering what I could.

The plan was to spend two days working with the children on lessons connected to fruit, vegetables and cooking and then have them make something the parents would eventually eat, all connected to English language, though the featured country wasn't England but Ireland. The approach was to hit language over the head with a hammer, which is to say they'd repeat a word or phrase over and over until a child either tumbled what was being said or never got it at all and it had to be explained in French first before attempting the English. Like most learners know and I recognised, it helped if they could see the words on the page so they could remember the associated sounds but I only had them for three days, not the five as before Christmas. We spent a while listening to the Police track 'Voices' and taught them the lyrics: "Voices inside my head, echoes, things that you said" in the hope they'd remember the rhyming scheme of the two lines long after they left the Centre. In The Police song they especially loved the "Cha!" bits and so a whole new avenue was opened up when we counted the eight "Cha'"s and they had to count numbers 1 to 8 in English in their heads. The final event was their acting as waiters outside the canteen relaying information about each new parental arrival in English, asking for requests: "Do you want the Menu?" "What do you want?" and then memorising the orders and relaying each order back to the kitchen staff that then compiled the order and returned it to each waiter and then each waiter would return the dish to the table with an "Enjoy your meal!" in broken English. 'Voices' was the finale with all the children running around in the canteen where the parents were assembled at tables, strongest at the front in the sense of those identified as being quicker to pick up the language and the instructions and stronger in self-confidence and a natural ability to lead the kids who forgot what they were supposed to be doing.

I returned to the primary school, as the Assistant English Teacher with an extended contract that lasted until the first week in July and also managed to mount two performances of my adapted Gaston shows done in England, as an English chef who made crepes. I was also allowed to select a dozen of the strongest young people and together we worked on some simple little sketches in English. The final event involved me putting in an extra day of work unpaid as my contract had ended a few days before, but for me it was a thrill to see what could be done with some good teaching, a bit of leadership and self-belief in kids nobody listens to.

Gauguin's friends Meyer De Haan and O'Conor spoke good English and read it, but Gauguin was hopeless and that effectively cut him off from many of the written theories and cultural ideas of the English-speaking world. It's not about one culture being superior to another. It's just sheer cold logic: 2 billion people conduct a 24 hour-a-day traffic of ideas in one language (English) and 200 million conduct traffic of ideas in French. Who has the most awareness to offer, the most knowledge?

My teaching contract ended in late June and I was out of a job in a foreign country but as jobbing artist/entrepreneur I'd learnt to think on my feet. I was Micawber. The good news was I'd managed to save enough money to buy a 15-year old Renault 19 but had saved nothing else. Poverty stretched ahead.

I spent most of my spare time in 2007 writing 'The Chiseller', memoirs I'd had of my life and work in England to get a perspective, but made nothing in theatre. I'd managed to persuade a teacher I barely knew to translate my short story called 'Confessions of a rock n roll star' and read out to a small audience in Weardale ten years before. It was translated into French but lacking an actor, no contacts for venues or rehearsal spaces, I'd forgotten about it. Writing didn't put food on ze table or fags in ze bouche.

I lived for the first year and a half in France out at Rochefort-sur-Loire in the converted windmill on a hill but there was absolutely nothing going on after 8 pm. It was also a good 20-minute drive to the centre of Angers and I knew I had to have access to the city to stand any chance of being able to make theatre but that had to wait for at least another year. Meanwhile, I had survival to think about.

In France in the summer, generally at the weekends, they hold events called 'vide-grenier'. Vide means 'empty' and a grenier is an attic, so 'attic emptying' is the best translation, but literally it means 'car boot sale' or 'yard sale'. Car boot sales in the UK have a reputation for being dismal affairs where shady characters sell shoddy tat. Well, there's shoddy tat in France as well but they generally can turn out some real gems. Lack of a job and income had suddenly made my situation desperate so I turned to selling at the *vide-greniers*. Despite all the theatre I'd written to over the years, I didn't even have the slightest trickle of earnings coming in as no one had published or bought me and I was struggling with the language and not getting any younger.

A friend's father had recently died and his house sold and emptied of its final belongings with a view to being thrown out.

Apart from *vide-greniers* and the odd antique shop, there are no real charity shops in France, so I gathered all this junk together, set up a stall, paid a couple of euros to the organisers and sold off what I had. At the end of the day I raised enough to put fuel in my car and buy some credit for my mobile, as well as a little food. It wasn't going to make me rich but it kept me going. I drove around all my friends' houses and asked them to donate any old crap they didn't want – books, records, shoes, postcards, old magazines, old paintings, ornaments, badges, hats, coats – you name it, I collected it. Then I found a brochure that listed all the *vide-greniers* around the region every Sunday and methodically drove to about a dozen over different Sundays. I'd arrive at the crack of dawn, queue up with the other vendors, pay for my pitch and then decamp from the car, set up my second-hand goods on some old table tops, pile it with my junk and wait. With sandwiches and a flask of coffee, I'd often spend the whole day there, sometimes getting soaked by sudden downpours (not very often) or baked by the sun or, if I was lucky, get a cool pitch in the shade of some trees. Some days I made peanuts, others I'd get lucky and sell all kinds of silly little things, making between 40 – 80 euros but with a car and a phone at least I could survive a little longer.

At the end of August I received a call from a language school in Angers to whom I'd sent a CV a whole year before. After an interview, I started with them at the end of August 2007, thirteen months since I'd first arrived in Angers. I've been with them ever since and, at the time of writing, am still with them, though would quit tomorrow if I could and devote myself to writing books and making theatre full time. I talk about the English language and how it works, I get paid and I go home. I love making theatre but I never had much security from it and though it's a demanding master and I'm an obedient pupil, giving too much at times, I survived on a pitiful income. What's demanded me of a teacher is simple enough: support, some guidance, some advice, a smile. I teach adults of all ages, persuasions and backgrounds and find myself drawing on many skills I've gathered up over the years with drama and theatre: pronunciation, clarity, brevity, grammar knowledge, creative writing and tons and tons of patience. I also managed to pick the grapes again this year for the same chateau as the previous year but as a part-timer. There was no romance this time – only sweat, toil and mud.

Within a couple of months of getting to grips with this new security, I'd finished 'The Chiseller' and edited it ruthlessly so I could get to 'Gauguin' at last. I think the ruthlessness of my editing-as-an-exercise passed into 'Gauguin' and I went through it rapidly, removing almost all the other characters save for his or putting speech marks around what they said, trying to find a way to slip from one to another without confusing the audience. The original hadn't changed since 2003 and then 2005 when actors from The Actors Centre in Newcastle had read it as part of a public reading but it was a sprawling epic then and pitted with old-fashioned devices.

There was no central location in Angers where I could find actors. The best I could hope for was to see other shows, find actors whose work had something original and then approach them independently. In Angers I wasn't only an unknown quantity but a foreign unknown quantity who, in an effort to convey himself as an articulate, intelligent theatre artist, often fucked it up by drawing on the vocabulary available to an 8-year old French child. But I hadn't moved to France to be like so many British immigrants that came and lived in little colonies, rarely integrating with the natives, rarely learning the language. I felt a kind of freedom – it's the one place nobody judges me on my accent. The French don't hear a Geordie accent, only an English accent.

In June 2007 I was invited to do some stand-in work as Demetrius for an amateur production of 'A Midsummer Night's Dream' at an expensive spread in a nice village outside Angers, organised by the Anglophone Library. For a few hours I found myself back in Little England, except it wasn't North East England, more like Kensington, a place where accents akin to royalty filled the air. As soon as I opened my mouth I just felt out of place. I've worked hard to integrate since I moved here and can count only a few native British settlers as my friends - the majority are French. I can understand 90% of what's said and respond and talk with about 60% success, though that 60% is not perfect, simply an ability to 'bungle through' and be understood in principle. So it was that I bungled through my original Gauguin and found a way to free up the language so it all fitted into my mouth.

One of the best ways to make great theatre is probably *not* to have a budget. It sounds naive but there's logic to it. If somebody says to you: "Here's a ton of money to spend on costumes and set" then wouldn't you actually go out and spend it on costumes and a set? I did this with 'Cyrano' in 2001: they gave me £2K for the set and costumes and that sapped the need for invention. Peter Brook said all we really needed was an empty space and he was right. But I'm not him.

What criteria to decide what to keep and what to delete? I didn't want to repeat myself and I wanted to be pure in that I wanted to keep what felt right and chuck what didn't. My aim was to find ways to compare Gauguin's artistic drives, inspirations, poverty and meandering paths – through money-earning jobs, finding an original voice and struggling to make ends meet whilst keeping the dream alive despite rejection by many - to my own. But I hadn't come all this way to perform Gauguin in English and appeal only to ex-pats or English-speaking tourists and I didn't want to marginalise myself and create a play that'd have no commercial appeal in France. I felt sure it'd be a fascinating experience for them to listen to something with a quaint English accent and deserved a hearing, and anyway, Gauguin was theirs, born and raised in France. What right did this Englishman have to come over and perform a show about their hero in a language they'd not understand?

I'd been experimenting with bilingual Shakespeare already in Angers, adapting my Shopping with Shakespeare concept to appeal to both French and English audiences with an actress

(Sylvie) and managed to source French translations of Hamlet and The Taming of the Shrew, as well as Queen Katherine of France and her maid Alice when the former tries to learn basic English from the latter to woo Henry V. Curious for a French onlooker: they can't fully understand but see how the tempo and tone reflect emotions. I understood what Juliet was saying in English even though her words are French! Sylvie performed the first half of Hamlet's "To be or not to be" in French and I finished it off in English and finally Puck's closing speech in 'The Dream', one sentence following on from another in alternate languages.

Given the success of the concept working in practise, Gauguin' would follow the pattern: read alternate paragraphs in both English and French. I was evidently English but by then I understood and spoke French. Why should I dress up as Gauguin or try to be him? Why should I sport a moustache and Breton costume? That was about as interesting as actors in Shakespeare's plays getting dressed up in medieval costume. I was from the North East of England, so after some reflection I had a slightly longer but slightly better title: 'Gauguin's ghost takes temporary possession of a man from the North East of England'.

6 – Gauguin responds

Elizabeth – Liz – met her two years ago next month at a gig in Camden, a charity gig for AIDS. We saw Micro Disney. My friends didn't turn up so I was drinking alone, shaped into a quiet corner to smoke a J I'd rolled in the bog. I watched her dance – so lithe, so happening. She was a perfect coffee colour, coming over from Barbados in '67 as a baby she said. Except she wasn't a baby anymore – she was fucking magnificent: dreads down her back, big brown eyes, full lips, amazing white teeth, massive tits and an ass like a wild stallion. We started dancing to reggae and took it from there. Moved in together up on the top floor in Wilmington Square and for a little while everything was cool until the day we drove up to Hatfield to see a friend and on the return trip she pulled the car over behind a milk float and turned off the engine.

"What's up?"

"I'm going to have a baby,"

"Are you sure? Do you want a baby?

"Yes. No. I don't know."

We drove home in silence and she cried all night and refused to let me near her. Next day she packed and moved out with the help of her brother Jake who, a few days later, came to visit me with a stark threat.

"She doesn't want to see you again!"

"Why not?"

He set his angry face an arm's length from mine and said: "Do you know what my family is gonna do to you when they see a white baby in my sister's arms?" I remember thinking: Oh fuck – this is it, the big moment. I'd expected better. But then I thought: "Yeah fuck it, I don't care either!" But I did, of course. But I didn't chase her. I got fucked up for a bit to drown my sorrows and then went out and bought a ticket for Tel Aviv.

It makes me angry still, as a memory, but nothing's that important to get hung up about, better to channel the positive: the boy who sat here a year ago is a stranger to the man who sits here now, my friend, a stranger! Hippy philosophy might

sound naïve and clichéd like kids talking but at least kids keep
dreaming.

I jump on a bus, any bus and head back to the West End with a
question inside: is there anything here worth sticking round for?

In Oxford Street the traffic grinds to a halt so I get off and go
into Soho side streets and pass nervous men nipping out of the
shadows, sparkling piggy eyes stabbing at the top shelf. Does
your wife know you're here? Do you take the moral high ground
in the public eye? Is your life so dull? It's new to me yet it never
made more sense, since I got back. I used to be like that. I am
still. Outside a fag shop a billboard of Time Out, caption:
'What's in and what's out' Inside: a list of faces, music, clothes,
fashions, faux pas and trivia judged by some asshole.

"You people in Europe, you believe in nothing!" said the Arab
on the farm I worked on outside Tel Aviv.

In Regent's Park there's a nurse pushing an old man around in
a wheelchair and another nurse pushing a baby around in a
pushchair.

"Did you ever do anything special?" I want to say to the old man. *"Did you ever feel anything? Did you change the world or did you just take, take and take?"* It's in my mind but I don't say it.

* * *

On 2nd January 2008 I made my first visit to Pont-Aven, Brittany, for the first time in well over a century. Hanging round The Louvre in Paris with Vincent, I overheard an American tourist tell how they were travelling up to Pont-Aven on the train that afternoon, so I whispered farewell to a snoozing Vincent, slipped into their ear and took up temporary residence in their grey matter for the course of the journey.

There's a tendency to think ghosts float everywhere tirelessly but that's just a lot of guff invented by storytellers. Vincent's ghost is a bit of an outcast because he ended it himself. It had been over a hundred years since he'd done the deed and when I'd left him in Paris he was *so* fed up especially once he realised just how long forever was. As a spirit I have a kind of right to adopt the living to get around.

Anyway, it was a freezing cold day but I'd soon drifted around the old place once again. It was a shock. I was gob-smacked to see a bust of myself in the market place, astonished they named streets after me and some of my long-dead friends, annoyed they used my name and face to sell their fucking cakes, biscuits, postcards, tea towels to promote tourism – staggered, astonished, annoyed and yet quietly flattered, in a perverse way. Pont-Aven, it appeared, still liked money; only the traditional dress was missing, consigned to postcards and annual pageants.

I was struck too at how busy it was with cars nose-to-tail and tourists traipsing around with empty faces and vacant stares, all searching for something that can't be found. For a second I saw the horses and carts again with my friends and the scowls of the locals who always distrusted us, taking our money and giving us the minimum of civility in return. Hotel Julia had been transformed into the Town Hall and Pension Gloanec into a newsagent's and though the Town's museum displays a handful of some of my original work, they were never anything to write home about. It was good to see the stuff by Emile, Schuff and De Haan again, so many memories!

I remember the last time I'd seen Pension Gloanec – the black and white borders to the wide central door and windows, over the door a crude painting of Pont-Aven. I can see her now Marie-Jeanne, head to foot in fierce black with that starched white Breton headdress fan on her crown. She knew nothing about art but everything about artists. And she stood no nonsense, protecting her maids Louise and Marie like a Mother Hen, keeping the place spotless and serving up fish soups, or scolding men who traipsed mud in from outside or brought 'city ways' into her presence. Everything had appealed to me about Pont-Aven: the racing river powering the mill wheels, the rocky streams teeming with salmon and trout, the savage coast and cliffs, the windswept grey countryside, children with thick clothes tending geese and cattle in small fields, menhirs and dolmens embedded into the earth by ancient civilisations, blocks of cottages pouring wood smoke from their chimneys amid the sudden flash of a green valley. I could remember too benches and tables either side of the door of Pension Gloanec laden with painters and tourists and various female friends, but rarely Bretons or villagers of Pont-Aven there - they had their own watering holes and kept themselves to themselves.

My room was under the roof on the second floor, always neat and tidy just as I'd been trained in the Navy and never forgotten. Often I'd arrive and the Danes and English or the Americans would already be here, but they'd stay in the posher Hotel Julia a little way up. I hated the Danes of course - they reminded me of how shittily they'd treated me in '85 when Mette's family had played their part in getting the Copenhagen Mafia to close down my exhibition. The English drove me potty with their chirping voices like twittering chickens and the Americans with their poor drawling French and naïve observations of the world, as if Pont-Aven was their private zoo and its inhabitants residents in cages, were beneath contempt: most hadn't even heard of Impressionism. They looked with shock and dismay at my work back then though gaga for the *principle* that the art of the painter must be divorced from common life and based on a classical style and they looked with fake astonishment at our work and nicknamed us the 'pests' so we retaliated with the 'firemen.'

The last time I remember looking at the frontage was late September 1894, leaving her new, smaller pension L'Ajonc d'or, as she'd closed the Gloanec. Laid-up for almost four months with my busted leg I'd eventually sent Anna the Javanaise ahead to Paris but at that point had no idea she'd rip me off and do a runner. They warned me about her in Pont Aven. Nobody liked her; she was rude to everyone. Too trusting, that was my problem. Anyway, they'd helped me up onto the cart as I couldn't get up there myself – too pissed, had to be to bear the jolting journey up to Concarneau railway station in the back like a side of beef - as I couldn't handle being upright for more than a few minutes. Almost horizontal, the last thing I'd seen as we moved was the upper part of the pension and ghostly faces in upstairs windows had watched me like a prisoner on a tumbril headed for the gallows. I could have sworn they were laughing: "See, foreigner, that's what you get for flaunting yourself in our town!" Six months after that I was on my way to Tahiti.

As for January 2008, I'd soon found my American host tiresome and was looking for an opportunity to skip him for somebody more interesting when he'd gone to the site of Hotel Gloanec. I expected to find the dining room fire lit and Madame Gloanec with coffee and bread, but instead I found a brightly lit newspaper shop – one large room where there used to be two. I hardly recognised it.

Later on he drifted up to the Hotel Julia and was just moving gently from framed photograph to framed photograph on the wall, when I heard the door open and saw Mr Stowers enter the room.

I think you could use some help, I suggested and leapt from the American's right ear over to Stowers' left ear and into the cranium.

"Ok, but don't fuck me about. The amount of times I've been fucked over by timewasters is enough to drive most men round the bend."

I've already explained that I gleaned from Mister Stowers that it was in this small town that he'd set his heart on performing. I thought he was mad. It certainly wasn't Paris and he'd not be attracting reviewers but he hoped his audiences would be made up of locals and tourists mainly, a mix of English-speaking and French, as well as various other nationalities. His thinking was: my art wasn't the topic of the day for those who thought of entertainment as getting pissed, going to discos or lying on beaches so a visit to the number one inspirational hotspot for experimental Impressionism just had to be reserved for the more enlightened of the world and theatre featured on the list of 'Things to do for the enlightened' surely? On top of this was the fact that, apart from the gallery exhibitions and cafes, there was nothing to really keep the tourists in Pont-Aven once they'd taken their photographs and bought their biscuits.

This had all been in Stowers' memory and this was the logic he applied to justify his thinking but after that first visit to Pont-Aven in January 2008 and being too busy finding a new flat in Angers where he lived and working as a teacher, he wasn't able to do much about it. By the time June and July of 2008 had come and gone it was simply too late he'd missed the impetus. Nonetheless, partly as a brain exercise and partly as an exercise to see how to slim it down, he started learning lines in English.

There's nothing quite like it to help a writer slim his projected piece down to something manageable. They never tell you things like this in 'writer's school' and I can speak with some authority on the subject because I never really understood that until I got into his mind. Yes, it's time-consuming to learn 12 pages of text and repeat it over and over, refining what's spoken, looking for ways to link logic or the flow of thoughts, omitting what sounds good when written in imagination but in the cold reality of day and as a collection of syllables coming out of the mouth and into speech, sounds clumsy and pointless. It takes sacrifices to make something work. You need to go back to Pont-Aven and reassure yourself there's some help on the ground and an audience or you're fucked, I advised him.

"Thanks but it's me that's gotta fork out the petrol money and drive for eight hours. All you do is to sit with your feet up."

He decided to return to Pont-Aven and speak again to the one contact there disposed to talk: the Tourist Office, needing to hear that tourists inhabited the town between certain dates and then he'd make a pitch for a room next summer. I could have told him that, about the tourists – that's why I got out and went to Le Pouldu in 1889 and '90.

"Shall I do the show in French or English?"

French – the French are rubbish at English.

"And the English are rubbish at French."

So he decided to do the show in mostly French and partly English. As a man from the North East of England he'd be more natural in native English and able to appeal to English-speakers and as a resident of France and a speaker of French, he'd be understood by the French and retain some commercial appeal in the country where he hoped he'd be able to sell his work.

In March 2008 he moved out of Rochefort-sur-Loire and into a small, comfortable flat in the middle of Angers.

The major ambition in his life has always been to write new works and then get them into presentable shape for the public, as well as compile all into a body of work. Even in the luxury of the world of well-funded and professional theatre that's an enormous task - in his world it seems monumental, if not impossible. But he's persisted. He can at least say that with nearly all he's written and managed to get to the performance stage, he's done reasonably well in the hope that one day he might be able to present those completed works in a format sale-able to the world. Those with agents and publishers and one or two breaks, those with contacts, those who've invariably made progress on the national and international scene, can make such statements as: "I then presented my next work" sound so easy.

But for a 40+ single man, with little financial reward for sacrifices over the years, that is: a man who never spent a great deal of his time trying to impress, statements like this are nigh on impossible. But he's passed the point of no return, there's no way back and he still works hard to keep afloat.

With any move there comes expenses and he had to furnish his new flat, but at least he was in the centre and that gave him access to culture and theatre. It also gave him access to book shops, photocopy shops, libraries and, finally a whole host of potentially new venues. It was the work he did with 'Shopping with Shakespeare' that first set him off in the direction of thinking about alternative and interesting venues for 'Gauguin' as he wanted to try to continue this idea of performing theatre in non-traditional theatre spaces.

What about performing in an art gallery?

"I'm on the case, P."

'Shopping' was designed to be 'promenade', something he'd tried to do back in 2004 when he wrote and directed 'One of the Lads' at The Buddle in Tyneside and by adapting the same presentation and by performing Gauguin in an art gallery he'd be welcoming those who wanted to see theatre to also cast a glance at painting and art in general, inviting those who were interested in painting to witness a theatre performance.

In the first half of 2008, the closest he got to theatre was working with a selected bunch of students on his adaptation of Francis Veber's French play and film 'Le Diner de Cons'. Some years before, in England, he'd sat down one afternoon and written out, character-by-character and line-by-line by studying the English subtitles on the video and continually pressing PAUSE, the lines of 'Le Diner de Cons' by Francis Veber (Steve Carell and Paul Rudd starred in 'Dinner for Schmucks' in 2010, a US adaptation) and preserved the copied work in a notepad. Early spring 2008 he saw a chance to finally get it to some sort of workable state. It wouldn't be a full performance by professional actors but part of the way. He spent a few days typing up his scribbled notes into a script and collected together five actors/students. There were in fact more than five needed but he only had his volunteer group for 2 hours rehearsal every week and only six such weeks to get something into a presentable form.

Some characters were able to grasp the dryness of the comedic lines and some weren't. They weren't actors - it was a language school, not a stage school and the goal was to give them a learning experience. The instructional language of the operation was in English and they'd benefit from learning new words, vocabulary and pronunciation within the text. It was a useful experience and he managed to get at least the first 24 pages of the total 56 trimmed down to a presentable and compacted state. I just sat back and let him get on. The reading went well and round about the end of June 2008, with a small audience of students. Stowers led the piece so the others would have that strong central vein to hang securely onto while they themselves worked in their own characters. They got laughs. Laughs are good.

By July and August he'd managed to get 'Gauguin' into a solid English script and started learning the lines. He'd no dates booked and no goal at the end of it but he knew, having been reminded of the fact by 'Le Diner de Cons', that a script needed to be stretched and worked in the actual mouth of the speaker at the same time as being written. Writing in the imagination is one thing, making those imagined words sound plausible is another. To say he went out and worked his lines every day for two months doesn't sound as demanding as it should, I know that, but he did. Every day for two months equals sixty. He'd be out for at least an hour, so that was at least sixty hours non-stop recital: two and a half days total and all unpaid. He'd walk in the nearby Avenue Jeanne D'Arc in Angers, a tree-lined avenue of Hansel and Gretel-type houses built around servants' quarters and former stables that once housed the *bourgeoisie*. Free of traffic, he sought quiet anonymity to speak his lines aloud. Little-by-little, day-by-day, he worked and reworked the words and lines, often going back to his flat and slicing out sentences or entire paragraphs in an effort to get to the absolute core of the story. He had to decide too which characters not to mention at all for fear they'd clutter up the drive of the story and how to reposition words to give them a more natural effect in delivery. A great deal of Emile Schuffenecker was lost because of that. I found it painful: *your* deciding who to keep in and who to leave out of *my* life.

"I know you did. That's why I asked you to go fishing on those days and let me get on with it."

Every day he'd re-paginate, go to the photocopy shop and print off the latest edition and then go out again and read the new lines, going through seven different versions in this manner and gradually compacting everything down from its original 20 pages to 12. He wanted a delivery that was well paced and snappy, something that recalled me in my former witty and vibrant glory before ill-health, injury, alcoholism and clap reduced me to a fucking wreck, and also a script that allowed him to move between moods by facial expressions, things that can't be written.

In October 2008 he returned to Pont-Aven for two days with his friend C and was able to take some time to look at some possible spaces. The first they saw stared him in the face as the 'one', if only because of its name – Salle Gauguin. It's almost the first place any visitor to the centre of Pont-Aven sees, a compact room under the Town Hall but what, a hundred years ago, was actually a respectable hotel and restaurant owned by its patron, Madame Julia. What's now Salle Gauguin was, back then, the kitchens and cellar while a few doors down was Pension Gloanec. Salle Gauguin was in 2009 the local *salle des fete*, in French this means 'room of parties' but to an English-speaker translates as performance space or village hall.

It was this trip to Pont-Aven in October that convinced him the summer of 2009 would be the best time to launch the new show.

One of the advantages at working for a language school is that he got to meet, teach and get to know all manner of professions. So it was that one of his students, CL, who was studying English so that he could go to England, had a girlfriend, AU, who translated. He sent her the compacted English 'Gauguin' version by email and within six weeks she'd returned it, finished. He'd also managed to persuade a teaching colleague to come to his flat and give his script the once-over and so he had two complete versions: one in English and one in French. He supposed all that then remained was to create a third Gauguin, which was to be made up of interlocking paragraphs in English and French, starting off with French and when this newly translated French script was shown to him he naturally assumed it was perfect and ready for performance but when I saw it I groaned. Mistakes everywhere!

"How do you know?"

I just do. Poor girl's been working blind. She's done her best but it's not her fault.

AU had translated what he'd written in English but translation isn't that simple: he should've been sitting alongside her as she worked so he could've reminded her of the thinking behind each word and sentence. He'd used a lot of idioms that didn't translate because we French use different idioms and also because he wasn't able to show her how the narrative moved in and out of different tenses: present, past simple, present perfect, future, continuous, direct speech, reported speech and so on. It was easy for him to make sense of it but for her, working alone in her room, it was like she'd been translating in the dark. He'd hoped getting it translated would have been an easy process and he could immediately start learning the lines but the script at that stage fell short of what sounded natural. Effectively, his French script was, in French terms, as basic as it had been a year previous in English when he'd cut it down from the sprawling multi-role epic to a one-man show. It was to go through this revision process at least twice more with other friends before it approached performance state. But by then he had to start pushing 'Shopping with Shakespeare' forward instead - getting the show about my life put on would have to wait until after Christmas.

He'd made contact with a local actress Sylvie who'd produced and performed three one-woman shows of her own and managed to persuade her to be in Shopping with Shakespeare 4, wanting to perform it at the chateau of Angers, a magnificent castle with high walls, a drawbridge, 13 towers and a deep moat, but it wasn't possible at that time because the chateau on principle only allowed unpaid amateurs to perform there. Angers used to be the ancestral heart and administrative headquarters of the English Plantagenet family's domination of northern France for much of the 12[th,] and 13th centuries so 'Shopping' would have some appeal and so he set about cultivating contacts with venues similar to those in North East of England: hospitals, libraries, museums. But he failed, partly because they lacked imagination, partly because of his self-consciousness over his limited vocabulary. Despite an arsenal of translated documents explaining the concept (and references on www.youtube.com), he was met with blank smiles. It didn't make him angry but it made him feel sorry for Jacques Publique. He put together a video example of the concept and burnt 50 DVD's then sent them out to various addresses around the region. If the DVD examples had turned up wrapped in flashy silver packaging by express delivery to be signed for and featured glossy, stunning photographs, websites and interactive films featuring presentations in French and English by film stars *maybe* they'd have been falling over themselves to touch the hem of his denim jacket. But, like most people in the world, few want to accept that what sits in front of them - a middle-aged English man with a bad accent, poor command of French, worn training shoes and cropped haircut - can possibly be possessed of the image of 'intello'. I know how that felt.

Even his attempt to get some funding from the local town hall was met with a "stonewall" but he'd been down this road before in the UK and knew what he was capable of. He didn't feel any strong need to prove it. I mean, think about it: how many people in the world do you know would walk into a town hall and claim to be able to do certain things with theatre and NOT deliver? It's by this peculiar philosophy we managed to preserve our sanities as artists. You'll notice as I go on that I'll start referring to him and I as a joint 'we' – I mean it's hard to avoid this, the two of us getting all jumbled up but who cares? We managed to persuade the local Tourism Office to take the show in their interior space and then the Anglophone Library, run and stocked by Americans, offered their space, but there was no money from either venue so managing to persuade them was relatively easy.

Sadly, in France the system of funding can seem slightly medieval, like something from the long-forgotten Royal Court of Personal Favours. Let's be everybody's friend? No thanks. Neither Stowers nor this celebrated narrator wants to be everybody's friend. We want to tell some kind of truth with art and we can't do that and be everybody's friend at the same time. Being everybody's friend might be good for politics but it means you have to watch your p's and q's and you can't tell the truth or drop bombshells. Bombshells blast cosy ideas to smithereens and art should be dangerous. So, if the Northern Boy and I are square on one thing, it's that. *'Spectacles de la rue'* (street theatre) dominate France, partly because of the predictably pleasant weather but it's largely lightweight stuff: visual and musical, clowns, puppets or acrobatic displays indicative of the French *comédia* tradition that comes from a country where circus skills are prized. But T's head is still firmly rooted in the John Osborne's, Harold Pinter's, Sarah Kane's, Edward Bond's, Howard Brenton's and Mark Ravenhill's of this world. At their roots they had guts and didn't try to be everybody's friend – they couldn't because if they had they would never have broken free enough to be honest. Genius is a door-to-door salesman who, once in a blue moon, sells you something you *really* need. I dig that. I dig that. My 'Vision After the Sermon' changed *my* world.

Stowers managed to create an 'association' (a non-profit making small company) though he'd been reluctant: French administration is daunting at the best of times, even for the French, but for non-native speakers it's like a mountain of miscomprehension and misunderstanding. In England he simply declared himself self-employed and with this status was able to go about his business as: 'Tony Stowers – freelance artist', after all, it was the culmination of what he'd always wanted to put on his passport since 1981. In France he was expected to be in a classifiable group. Well, joining any kind of gang has always been anathema to him (and me), so we'll generally do the minimum required by law and spend the rest of the time kicking in the teeth of conformity. But he had to belong to something so he became Compagnie Tony Stowers because everybody else became Compagnie Blah Blah Theatre, which limited what he felt able to do.

Vis-à-vis Pont-Aven, following up my suggestion to perform in an art gallery, he'd phoned through a polite request from Angers to meet somebody from a small international art school to discuss performing alongside student exhibitions in January 2009, being told he'd be contacted by the end of the month. Two months later he still had no response so he drove up to Pont-Aven and, from the local Tourist Office, managed to place a call to the Principal or Director in question, mentioning he was 50m away and could he pop in and discuss his proposal as he'd driven 250km? She was too busy. Now, if that'd been me I'd have barged in, picked her up by the scruff and slapped her round the fucking chops. Luckily for her, it wasn't me. He bore it with dignity and patience and I admire him for that.

He eventually met her in the same room I'd slept in, in Pension Gloanec (her private office), in early March on another visit there when he'd come with the intention of booking Salle Gauguin.

"Well, I thought you might 'ave gathered if we 'adn't responded to you we simply weren't interested?"

He replied as politely as he could that he wasn't a mind reader. And she had the nerve to say this in Pension Gloanec – my fucking bedroom! You see? We were both rejected by Pont-Aven, in different ways.

I was at least happy to see some original Impressionist stuff hanging in the gallery from my old mate Emile Schuffeneker and me!

"Why don't you put your show on here?" I suggested, "It's ideal."

"I'm way ahead of you," he said.

He spoke to the Receptionist and asked if it'd be possible to meet the Director as he'd travelled from Angers and a return visit would be difficult in the immediate future. The difficulty was when they wanted to know: "What's it about?" He'd the same problems in England: you can't just tell a receptionist you want to put a theatre show on in their gallery. They'll pass on the message in the most basic manner possible, as they pass a million similar messages on everyday. What the artist needs is a chance to pitch an idea.

In France his limited vocabulary made it more difficult to explain how much he needed to meet face to face and walk through the concept and then if they still didn't like it *then* they could say no. Unfortunately the Director of the Museum exhibiting the aforesaid work was the same as the Director of the small art school: as soon as he mentioned the word theatre she automatically shifted into 'Send a letter' mode, not even a chance to meet her or test the waters with the idea. Two rebuttals in an hour? Ouch.

Reluctant as he was to gamble 500€ of his own hard earned on the hire of Salle Gauguin (85€ a day for six days), he had to secure it to keep to the deadline. I think it was about then C noted: "They don't want you in Pont-Aven", but he chose to ignore that by adding (and I admire it): "I'm doing it for Gauguin".

True enough, there was negativity from some in Pont-Aven but he refused to be beaten, *we* refused to be beaten. These negative reactions were against the spirit of what he thought we stood for. That wasn't to say others were wrong in their judgements but the manner in which they made their judgements made both of us angry. Their decisions were made on a: 'I know better than you' basis and of course that was bollocks because most of the time we hadn't even got to the pitch, so they didn't have a clue what we wanted. As far as I could see, little had changed in that part of France since the last time I was there in 1894. This aloofness still rules decision-making civil servants in France.

Learning lines in French is tricky. When learning lines in English you look at the words and read them until their meanings and sounds gradually imprint onto the memory. In English he knows what each and every syllable is doing in its correct place and how it makes up every single word and with a meaning he's completely sure of and recognises. Whereas in French he finds himself stumbling across words he doesn't know or, if he does, it's in a different form, as verbs change their endings depending on the time they're being used in or whether or not the goal of the noun is masculine or feminine. We French simply can't use language in the same way you English use it. I should paraphrase that: we CAN but we're not used to language having its own will. You English pride yourselves on an individualism reflected in your language. For the French, language is a slave to our feelings, meanings and intentions and is largely a passive servant. Stowers needed to know the *exact* pronunciation of every single word in the French parts of his script because if he didn't, he'd memorise it in its mispronounced form and his final delivered text would be punctuated throughout by tiny errors. Those tiny errors could easily misrepresent his intention or send the listeners off into areas where the language shouldn't have led them. He knew the exact meanings and sounds of all the words in the English parts of his script and learning them was relatively easy because more often than not they were little flags that represented certain logic in the narrative. But in French, his English logic was often so strong that it'd conjure up French words to represent his English ones and lay them out in the wrong order: right words, wrong order of delivery, yet another way in which the French audience can be misled or sent off in the wrong direction. He had to fight against the handful of translators who shaped his work into French to maintain a sense of British sarcasm and subtlety, rather than be obvious. An effective way to learn the lines seemed to be to record the French version to digital minidisk and listen to it over and over on CD, but then he found himself trying to imprint sounds on his memory rather than words and, for some inexplicable reason, it was like being on ice, constantly falling, slipping and sliding.

Another difficulty was trying to make what was on paper sound like natural speech. It was under constant revision as he read his skeleton script aloud every day, starting from early April, fine-tuning, deleting odd words that seemed to break up the rhythm of a sentence or phrase, even letters in some cases. He might add words too, to try and connect one idea with the next, showing how the character's mind is moving in certain directions as he both diverts the flow of his thoughts and allows his thoughts to be diverted - do we control what we say or do our memories dictate what we will say? Do we speak from a foundation of analysed logic or rationality or do we react to instinct?

He had to find the correct places to stress lines. English is a stress-led language, unlike French. However, once he was able to identify where the stress of a line was in English, he then had to find the equivalent place in his newly-translated-into-French line. With English the stress could, for example, be on the word "me". In French and in the past tense this word is reduced to one letter followed by an apostrophe (m'). That looks odd to his eye (though not to mine) and it takes a while for his occipital to automatically click in with stress under what is only a one syllable sound – 'm'.

After about three weeks of reading, he tackled a re-write (dubbed 'Gauguin Experimental') and made pencil changes. On a daily basis as a teacher he used his own form of phonetic alphabet to help students understand how to pronounce correctly: 'taught' and 'brought', for example, the past of 'teach' and 'bring', are often pronounced 'tosht' or 'brofft' by lower level students because nobody has explained to them that the real sound is more like 'torte' and 'brorte' - he wrote these last two on the board of his language school on an almost daily basis to help students understand pronunciations. He employed this crude system to rewrite 'Gauguin Experimental'. Some French sentences proved simply too difficult to get a hard, flat English tongue around. The French tongue literally dances in the mouth or produces sounds formed more by the cheeks, we French don't use many facial muscles to get the best out of sound. For example, the sentence: "Je savais qui si j'étais reste il m'aurait tué" (I knew if I'd stayed he would have killed me, written for me to describe why I had to leave Vincent alone in Arles just before Christmas 1889) he rewrote as "Je savvay kee-see jay-tay restay, il moray two-ay". To an English and French eye this is gobbledegook but to a French ear this means something, so once he'd rewritten the new phonetics he wouldn't hesitate as his logic searched for significance in the weird assortment.

From January 2008 onwards he also began a regime of scrimping and saving. This was something I could relate to – you learn to be self-managing. If you're famous and rich you can pay accountants to take care of that end but if you're a chiseller you get to do your own books and it's not easy - all around you lay the temptations of the material world but you daren't touch. You gamble. You put aside what you need to live on and clothe yourself and spend what's left on paints, brushes, canvasses, booze and the next meal. His car, an old thing in constant need of upkeep and repair, struggled on without hubcaps, dents, balding tyres, moth-eaten electrics, half-torn bumper and a smoky engine that spluttered and coughed if left out on cold nights. No extravagances, doing his best to ensure that at the end of every month he was able to pay the bills and put something aside to pay for the publicity for the show.

At the start of March he resurrected 'Confessions of a rock n roll star' for four performances over two nights in a cellar bar in Angers and spent about 100€ on posters and flyers, trudging around the centre of town placing them. Give me a silver dollar for every mile Stowers walked between 1981 and 2009 getting posters put up and I'll be the richest ghost in Europe. Total audience came to about 20. He'd canvassed almost a hundred people, half of them students and people who worked at his language school, but most were too busy. So, after this temporary interruption it was back to Gauguin.

By mid-April, he'd drawn up an impressive list of all possible images or other paintings that could be used in the show and arrived at 30. That meant 30 frames. I wanted to help but despite being the creator of almost all of them, they were in the hands of private collectors around the world or locked away in museums or vaults. After a little more understanding of the quality related to the density of memory in each digital image did he understand not all the thirty would be of sufficient quality to copy so that number was revised to fifteen. I'd already sold them (or they'd been inherited by my family) after I surrendered my worldly flesh in 1903 so there was no financial benefit to me but Stowers and I came from the same shoestring-budget-upbringing mentality. There were cheap stores on the edge of Angers where he could buy frames but they *looked* cheap so he toyed with the idea of tracing them all from *vide-greniers* but the downside would be that they'd all be different shapes, some beautiful, others ugly. Should we care about the uniformity of the frames or throw caution to the winds and plaster the performance wall with a tapestry of frames?

Furthermore, he still had no place to stay in Pont-Aven for the show and started to worry about extra costs for B&B or camping. Chances were he was going to be alone for the trip (apart from me) but my role was limited: I could influence, but I couldn't operate the machinery or carry lights, drive or set up tents! Somebody had to sit at the door to take tickets but who?

Meanwhile, in early March the Tourist Office in Pont-Aven had given him the name of a man who ran Museum Paul Gauguin in a warehouse on the edge of town; it hadn't been around in my day. The second time we'd driven to Pont-Aven we'd noticed it – a sprawl of emptiness bearing my name. I didn't realise I'd lived such a full life to take up so much space. Stowers had phoned from Angers and been told by a 'Secretary' that he'd be more than welcome to look at their Museum as a possible venue so we went with enthusiasm but when we got there were shown a completely empty building.

It began to occur we were actually dealing with people who had ambitions for a museum but no support from Pont-Aven and were treated as eccentric but that could have been and probably was just small town snobbery. Having always been a fan of the outcast, I wanted Stowers to pursue the connection but he wasn't sure. The 'Director' (Mr Le Farge) at the totally empty Gauguin Museum had asked him to compile a list of questions about my life, so Stowers could double-check events and dates. Even if he could have sat down and asked me to clarify events and dates from my first-hand accounts I'd have had real problems – it was so long ago and I was out of my head half the time, especially near the end thanks to that absinthe.

But T felt unhappy – Mr Le Farge was putting all the responsibility for fuck-up's back into his court; if T didn't ask the right question, Mr Le Farge would allow it to pass and T'd be putting something into the script that was an error. Small errors could be handled but missing out an event by, for example a whole year or even two, would look bad. Stowers hoped Le Farge would look and say: "You need to change this" etcetera. No such luck. After, they showed him a very dirty room he could use for the show and have for nothing provided he cleaned the place up and part-decorated it, at least three days work. T smiled politely, shook their hands and went back to Angers. A day later he sent Mr Le Farge email to the effect that he planned to return at the end of May and could spare some time then for lunch to talk about the script. But he never did. In the event he let Museum Paul Gauguin drop. I still today don't know how I felt about that.

"Does the expression 'flogging a dead horse' translate to French?"

He looked at renting a van for 9 days, transporting everything in the back and maybe sticking a mattress in and sleeping in it, not very comfortable but cheaper than a B&B.

We have President Sarkozy to thank, in a small way. In March 2009, due to the financial crisis of 2008, Sarkozy announced his intention to give 3.5m low-waged workers in France a one-off grant of between 200€ and 500€. In April, T received this boost into his account and it helped him get the publicity printed without putting him back on the breadline.

Can we have a rest now, T? I'm fed up of reading.

"Yeah, but no smoking!"

7 – Working together

I made my excuses, went outside, leaned over the gutter, vomited three pints of lager and a sausage sandwich, wiped my mouth and went back in to continue my conversation like nothing had happened. And it hadn't. Better to be rid.

Earlier that day I'd taken an Ecstasy pill and smoked I-don't-know-how-many-joints in my flat. Later that weekend I'd drink about two gallons of lager, take three or four more Ecstasy tablets mixed with LSD, piss everywhere except the toilet, shit my pants and crawl around on my hands and knees begging for forgiveness. I was almost 30. Maybe the best I could hope for was what everybody else in the world around me seemed to do: accept humanity in general wasn't very special after al, we're all just muscle for hire and the only thing worth doing was making money for the sake of it? I'd not done any acting for five years and I was haunted by the nightmare of that summer of 1988 so many things went wrong because I wasn't old enough or smart enough to know a good thing. I should've been a working actor by then with small breaks on the screen or writing sketches and performing them in alternative cafes, trying to entice BBC scouts to give me a break. Why was I pouring myself into a crumpled heap every night convincing myself I was worthless? I was a mess. Was I thick, uneducated working class Northern scum who'd never had even a grain of talent and had only been good for looking as if he had? I was a liar and cheat to those I conned money out of on the telephone and a liar and a cheat to myself for pretending I was something special. Or was I just playing the role? When does reality turn into entertainment? Somewhere in all this I'd managed to write plays and stories but there was little time for the luxury of sitting around writing – in London you needed to work ALL the time. I flogged ad space on the 'phone and got fucked up a lot. I hated myself but was too arrogant to admit it and the more I hated myself, the more I got fucked up. If I could have been assured back then that ending life was painless I might have read page one but I could never extinguish the hope that maybe one distant day I'd write about all this shit. They'd warned me in Darlington: "London will chew you up and spit you out when it's finished!" Or would it? Wasn't suffering all part of life's rich tapestry? Isn't there a cliché that says artists are supposed to suffer? Where was my crown of thorns, my crucifix, my Calvary? Time would tell.

* * *

On 2nd January 2009 I quit smoking. I'd been a veteran smoker for 25 years, despite three previous attempts to stop. I don't remember (or care to remember) how many times I'd stocked up on the evil weed, having my lungs munch through it until my brain was a mere onomatopoeic squelch, but there I was living in student accommodation at 46, with a tapestry of work behind me but poor as a church mouse, cherishing and clinging onto my dreams with ne'er a pot to shit in and no bog roll, knowing if I lost my job tomorrow I'd be begging on a street corner within a month. Knowing the risks, I'd just get fucked for a few days on end. Bliss.

"Why did you spunk it all for booze? You'd have lasted for years and reaped all the benefits if you hadn't."

You need talk, Mister Perfect! Self-discipline, pal - to get in shape for Pont-Aven – it's a state of mind. I coughed up oil slicks but found a fighting spirit and instead of putting cigs in my mouth started putting in fatty foods, chocolates and sweets instead and the pounds (or kilos) piled on but getting into shape wasn't the last resort of a middle-aged man trying to look sexy; it was to be light on the toes. I'd committed to three shows a day for seven consecutive days, every performance had to be different and exhausting and I didn't want to go away feeling I'd not given 100%.

Apart from Gauguin I'd also been pushing to get Shopping with Shakespeare off the ground. 2009 was the 600th anniversary of the birth of King Rene of Anjou and a number of celebrations were planned to commemorate his birth. After producing a bilingual Shopping with Shakespeare 4 the previous November, I was confident Angers would want to celebrate the connection between King René and Shakespeare - René featured in a short scene in the first part of King Henry VI written to take place in front of the walls of the Chateau of Angers. It was made for the anniversary I thought.

I'd managed to cut a nice 'How Shopping with Shakespeare Works' DVD from 4 with French friends who gave up free time to help, spent about 200€ sending out the DVD's to 50 potential venues, asked a work colleague to help copy half of the DVD's on his Mac, spent hours researching addresses of chateaux, museums, galleries and finally universities and colleges, as well as various festivals and I didn't get one reply from 50+ DVD's posted out in January, nor an email and not even a phone call.

The same happened for 'Henry Jones – English Shopkeeper' the show to help French kids learn English. The 'Gaston' shows in the UK had been very popular and I'd performed each of them over 100 times. Again, with the help of French friends, I wrote and sent flyers containing 400 envelopes, 400 stamps and 400 double-sided A5 photocopies - and not one school replied. Not one phone call. Not one email. Every single one of them was waiting for a telephone call from me to ask if they wanted it and they may well have wanted it but wouldn't say yes or no until I phoned them and grovelled. This is how it is in France.

Having translated a great deal of general information from English to French in the previous months as a teacher and done a lot of editing with my own work, I'd also begun to wonder if maybe I'd lost a few important details in m Gauguin play? So I went back to the Internet and did a little double-checking on facts originally traced from books in Gateshead in 2003 and had some surprises - somewhere in those translations I'd erred and had a list of corrections to make, especially on dates and characters, but that little extra task fuelled my imagination and I added a final paragraph that kind of summed up how I felt: *Gauguin: The taxman, the Catholic Church and the colonial government all wanted to shaft me – three months in prison they gave me, me, a man in my state! Well, better to die a free man than to die a slave. This world treats its artists like shit. It makes them beg and struggle and kiss arse for pennies or for a loaf of bread and then the world takes their art from them and pontificates that genius is a curse and the artist must suffer on the cross like a reluctant Jesus - for their sins! And what are their sins? They jealously guard the sins of avarice and greed and stupidity and fear and wrap them up as generosity, benevolence, intelligence and courage, unable to find truth and beauty in their own lives. Every day of my life has been a war, a war between the positive and the negative, the strong and the weak. The strong are those who speak their minds and make no effort to be everybody's friend, but beware the weak, my friends – you can spot them easily: they are those who tell you: you cannot do what they cannot do themselves. For the weak are more concerned with what others think of them than what they think of themselves.*

"I like it. Especially those last two sentences. But you're a bit off the mark with a few facts."

I'd recorded in my original 'Gauguin', written in Newcastle in 2003, that an author called Viaud with the pen name of Loti, had written 'Loti's Exotic Travels in Polynesia.' No book of that name ever existed. 'The Marriage of Loti' was originally published as 'Rarahu' but there was no evidence his story was linked to a story of a sailor marooned on a beautiful island full of beautiful, naked women (the line I'd written). I revamped and suggested it was *interwoven* with the traditional sailor's fantasy story of the paradise island of legend populated by naked Amazons, the deserted island where many a storm-tossed sailor fearful for his life hoped he'd be washed up if his ship went down.

I drew up a list of single items to serve as props for each of the 13 characters – props that had something to say or contribute. But as soon as I jotted down 'walking stick', 'monocle' and 'crucifix' I had to remember the performance space was like a temporary art gallery and anybody who was there would be like most people in art galleries: expecting to see an exhibition, not a space set up for a theatre show. I'd be in amongst that crowd in modern dress and burst into life so I couldn't arrive carrying a walking stick and wearing a monocle and not be noticed, not in Angers anyway!

At least two of the characters appear twice, one three times –
Edgar Degas and Gauguin's estranged wife Mette - so I had to
figure out one or two physical or verbal features to define them,
so it was clear different people were talking. I also had to think
about the limp. In May 1894 Gauguin broke his ankle in a fight
at the nearby port of Concarneau and yet despite asking
'experts' nobody seemed to know whether he broke the left or
the right so as I'd always had trouble with my own left ankle
over the knees through various scrapes and drunken follies –
twice putting it in plaster with fractures - *I* decided.

"It *was* the left."

Are you sure?

"No. Maybe it was the right?"

You can't even remember which ankle you broke, T? Did it
mean I'd appear throughout the show with a limp? Having a
limp was about as artificial as having a walking stick or a
monocle.

In the week starting 18th May, the local newspaper Ouest France published an article about my plan to celebrate King René's 600th birthday. I'd done the interview six weeks prior in early April and hoped it'd have been printed early enough to use as leverage to get more bookings for Shopping with Shakespeare but the editor had decided to delay publishing until on the day of 27th June. But if I was going to use it as leverage to try and salvage more bookings for Shopping, I needed something in the paper ASAP.

The printed publicity for Gauguin was a big step: it'd started to become real, not that I ever doubted but it's always a strange time when you feel that transition taking shape. The journey to perfect it had taken longer than I'd hoped - every time I'd added or deleted a word on the screen, the printer, Jeremy, would print a copy on paper and look at it again. Impatience would get the better and I'd say: "It's done. No more", when it clearly wasn't. I hate having to reel in enthusiasm. I'd tried adding to the posters that for the entry fee of 10€ people could have a copy of the script in French/English. But each script was 11-pages long and how many people would come? How much more would it cost on top of my outlay? Would they be too busy looking at their scripts or rattling the pages to watch the performance? That idea fell aside. The script had odd words and phrases that families might find offensive. Could I add something that warned parents that it was best not to bring in kids under 12 but word it in such a way as to suggest there was nothing overtly shocking in it at the same time? Were these things regulated in France? How? Initially also there was too much explanatory text overlaid onto the split images of Gauguin's face and my face, blocking out both our features so I had to trim down. Original drafts had featured everything in French and English but it turned the poster/flyer into an ugly block of black text, so we had everything in French except one brief explanation on the front. The total print cost was 478€ for 200 full colour A3 posters and 1000 double-sided colour A5's. I wanted to distribute 1000 A5's to Brittany destinations for Pont-Aven and 1000 to distribute for the Angers gigs for which at the start of that week I still had to find a venue!

"You also managed to get all 11 pages of the script into your head about the same time. You can thank me later, T."

I'd struggled right to the very last line. I spent a lot of time going over the text and began to understand certain things about French grammar and pronunciation in that my memory had become fixed on certain errors I wasn't even conscious of making. Breaking down, reworking and perfecting them was slow and some neural pathways of memory in my brain were rockier than others.

Next challenge was to get the publicity up to Brittany to a distribution agency and send out a press release - more translations, more favours, more work and more time.

And finally, at the end of the month I visited Pont-Aven again with C. We took the old road from Angers to Nantes, which took an hour and then the long slog along the underside of the thick muscled arm that juts out into the Atlantic, also known as Brittany, parked near a pizza restaurant and had lunch. The tiny market was just wrapping up.

First, the Town Hall: I needed another viewpoint on the space. If I was going to charge 10€, the customers/audience needed to feel they were entering a space that justified their money. We established one corner of the large room would be best though for a long time I'd been labouring with the hope I'd make the show open, as in a promenade piece, using the entire space as a gallery, strolling around, but Salle Gauguin had too much wall space. A half-hearted job to fill it would have left huge breaks between my framed pictures. It also would have meant investing money in frames and the catches to hang them. I had to avoid hammering nails into the wall - if chipped or pulled out afterwards it'd leave marks and I'd forfeit my 100€ deposit. Luckily there were five moveable screens/blinds available, so they'd come in useful for blanking off the corner of the performance space. With another previous English one-man show Space Jockey, I'd performed in front of a bar behind the watching audience and been thrown by the visual distractions of the barman competing with my efforts to remember my lines. Going up onstage and winging it like a stand-up comedian just ain't the same as learning lines and repeating them.

We were going to need something on the floor as it was unwelcoming and the black colour absorbed the limited light. I used a pace-measurement to decide on 6 m x 4 m in the corner closed in on both outer edges of the carpet with two or three rows of chairs. I'd be performing on the same level as the audience so the chairs would have to be arranged to give good visibility. 6m x 4m meant we were looking at a front row on both sides of about 16 seats, a second row of 16 seats and a third row of the same. So the audience was now set at a capacity of 48 per performance. In the event it turned out to be 4m x 3m carpet because I couldn't fit a longer length into the car. This reduced the audience capacity to 27.

The previous Sunday I'd gone through my lines, sat down in a comfy garden chair and propped my head up with my elbow against a garden table. This position changed my delivery so voice and delivery was more calculated, whereas moving around made it more laboured. What about an armchair set in the centre of the carpeted floor with a small table nearby? But what was the purpose of the table? Everything on stage (like everything in a film or in a book) has to have a reason to be there. Was a table only going to be there to prop up my head from time to time or could it have other uses?

I'd been hoping that I could buy postcard size images of the works but that would have meant the actual images would have been very small - postcard-size, of course. For the audience to get any benefit from images so small they'd need access to the walls and in the original art gallery this would have been possible. But I was adapting to a performance space that wouldn't allow the audience to get up and cross to see the frames. I was going to have to use the Internet after all and draw down high memory images in full colour.

After being in Salle Gauguin for only about 15 minutes, I had a much clearer picture of what the eventual set–up would be - the actual problem of getting the equipment up there from Angers was further down the line. We returned the key and asked for a copy of the room rental agreement.

Our next port of call that day was just across the square to the tourist shops that sold postcards but it became clear none sold the postcards I needed. Our final call was the tourist office where my local contact received us with a smile and we met the man who'd distribute the Gauguin flyers and posters. Did we know about the campsite near Pont-Aven? We didn't. Was it important? Yes - around 3,000 English-speaking tourists stayed there in the summer. He thought it important and relevant but I was cautious. I still had the memory of depleted audiences with Space Jockey in London in 2004 and a £2K loss the show took.

The distribution company would send their bill (estimated at around 300€) when the job was done which could be late July. The previous week I'd taken delivery of the printed publicity but was only able to pay the printer 300€ of the 478€ bill. I still owed him 178€ and what with my rent going out of my account for May, I was paranoid about being out of pocket but then I've never made much money from my work anyway. To make real money you need a team of producers and agents.

After that there was nothing else for us to do in Pont-Aven and as it was a three-hour drive back to Angers we set off early, driving past the Museum Gauguin on the edge of town. Their Director Mr Le Farge had promised to help check my script and I'd promised to call him but I never did.

Some days I'd rigidly stuck to my self-imposed rule of reading the script everyday between early April right up to the first performance and other days I'd had to really force myself, especially late in the evening around 10 pm after returning from my job. A diary entry in late May: "It's coming up to 1 p.m. on a late May lunchtime and I'm going to go through the lines now before leaving the house in about an hour to go to the dentist. After that I'm going to work until 8 and then to the opening of a new exhibition, the one that may or may not be the space I need to bring Gauguin to Angers in the autumn. I doubt I'll have time or inclination later on today, so now is best. There's no feeling of robbing myself, that is: doing a half-hearted job - in some way, shape or form an extra syllable or an extra letter or word is registering itself in my memory every time."

I found a rehearsal space in Angers: lovely room, well lit, isolated, comfortable, used by other professional companies. I'd used it in March for 'Confessions of a rock n roll star' but if it wasn't insurance companies wanting to tie me down, it was the owners of the space (the Town Hall) themselves fighting to keep out undesirables or it was the Management of the space, a private theatre company.

After showing my new insurance status, I booked the rehearsal space from 1st – 8th August and signed. I needed to get into that space right up to before the physical move to Pont-Aven and work in the script with the props and the lights - what is imagined in the head is never the same as what happens with the set and lights in place. Imagining a prop exists and reciting the lines around it is quite different to actually having it in front of you. This sounds so obvious but writing it is my way of reminding myself how obvious it sounds and how easy it is to overlook the obvious. There's a saying in France *"Chacun sa merde!"* - "Everyone has to sort out their own shit", which is to say: "You're on your own – we had to struggle and so do you and though we were desperate when starting out, now we're established, we're not going to help you." This expression pretty much summed up my relationship with the company that managed the rehearsal space and became a later addition to Gauguin. Art imitates life!

8 – The plot thickens . . .

"I'm on the seacoast in a fishermen's inn near a village of one hundred and fifty. I live like a peasant and I work. I spend one franc a day on food and two sous for tobacco. I accept De Haan's money because I can do little else but when I look at the money I made hand over fist on the Stock Exchange . . . I produced nothing and was paid handsomely. Here I produce something beautiful but am ignored. My paintings and sculpture terrify everyone - they make a great sensation but are terribly difficult to sell."

"Writing to your wife, Mister Gauguin?"

I turn to see her standing at the door watching me. The wind and rain spit and howl outside. A log fire crackles in the grate. Around us the walls, window, ceilings and doors twist and turn with their golden images - the windows with studies of Breton life, the swan on the ceiling, below the window a quotation from Wagner condemning the artist who works for money, on the mantelpiece a bust of De Haan carved from oak flanked by decorated pots and on shelves each side statuettes of a Javanese dancer and a Negress. The top half of the door is covered with a copy of "Bonjour Monsieur Gauguin" and on the bottom half a portrait. The doors of a cupboard bear my self-portrait and a portrait of De Haan and in the centre of the wall is her large portrait - Mam'selle Henry by De Haan - with a frame I painted but its existence, I fear, has swelled her head.

"This inclement weather lacks inspiration, Mam'selle Henry."

I stub out my rolled cigarette and she holds the spoon over my glass, drops two sugar lumps onto it and expertly pours the absinthe, dissolving them. I swill it around once and knock it back in three. My gut shudders. She clumps across the wooden floor to the window and blocks it with her portly size. Wiping her hands on her apron she casts left and right.

"Jacob has gone down to the beach to look for crab and, Messieurs Seguin, Filiger and Chamaillard have gone to Quimperle for supplies."

Sharing Madamoiselle Henry's bed, Jacob is luckier than most – her girth keeps him warm at night. Serusier, Laval and Seguin are also lodging here but more fluid with their money supplies than I. So long as they pay their bills, I'm lumped in with them and safe as we all share the same heat from the fire and eat from the same pot. Seguin will never amount to much as a painter though – he's half-hearted. His only brave act in life was throwing in the towel on his job in law to bask in the shadows of the full-timers. He's a young man but I wouldn't count on him in a fight. I sense Seguin, Chamaillard and Filiger will all end their days paupers after sacrificing all and gaining no great insights. Chamaillard and Seguin have local friends, Laval and Serusier has enough to keep them and De Haan has a pension. I have zero. Poverty has to be experienced. It's a gradual, slow physical destruction through poor diet and cold and a psychological cancer in the constant guilt, an embarrassment, avoided by all but the desperate and the poor. King of the Penny Jugglers, I must wait like a servant until I'm offered a smoke, invited to a table to eat, passed down some old clothes. "I'm descended from the Borgias you know?" used to sound so impressive but now it only invites sarcastic jokes.

"Ah!" exclaims Mam'selle Henry, as the sun pokes through the clouds and sends a shadow of the hotel across the road outside.

We live a frugal life. We swim in the sea but it's usually cold. We talk endlessly, drink and smoke heavily and decorate everything we can lay hands on, from sticks to clogs, plates to chairs. In the evenings we play cards and draughts or work at the easel or we carve wood washed up on the beach. I play the guitar, adequately, the piano badly but then it's a bad piano.

"Mr Bernard has proposed I write letters to newspapers, articles. He says they pay well. Would you care to hear my efforts, Mam'selle Henry?"

"Why not?"

"Painting is the most beautiful of all arts. Like music it acts on the soul through the senses, the harmonious tones corresponding to the harmony of sounds, but a unity is possible in painting that one cannot obtain in music. Like literature, the art of painting says what it wants but says it all at once. When you listen to music or look at a painting you are free to dream. When you read a book you are the slave of the author's mind. Yet critics are always men of letters, who spend their time defending their own work as if a truly good work does not defend itself. To judge painting and music one must be a born artist."

"I think I'd prefer the letter to your wife," she says, looking me full in the eyes. I smile, see the challenge, realize what it is that attracted Jacob to her and why I admire her, having abandoned the life of a servant in Paris to run her own business out here on the edge of the world. It was her experience of city life that enabled her to cope with the notions of art and artists, for in Paris she knew they were important. Out here on the edge of the world, we are suspicious aliens to a Breton people carved from granite that only the relentlessly pounding ocean can wear away. And I'd fuck her – if she'd let me.

"Very well. "My dear, I will not give up my art. My business is art; my capital is the future of my children. The honour of the name I've given them will be of enormous value to them one day. My art is nothing at present but will stand out eventually."

"What kind of a man can abandon his wife and children to live as you do, Monsieur Gauguin?"

"What kind of a person can go through their entire life convinced they have nothing beautiful to offer the world, Mam'selle Henry?"

She looks at me for a few moments and says nothing.

"A letter came for you – Paris,"

She hands me the creased envelope. I open it. It's from Theo Van Gogh. Vincent has shot himself. Oh Vincent, now you've gone and done it . . .

* * *

Back in January 2009 he'd pictured the months ahead vaguely unrolling like a picnic: an easy job as a teacher, a stress-free life in his small apartment in quiet Angers, weekend visits to the countryside with friends and the only challenge being the lines once a day.

A balmy Anjou summer arrived in early May but only in June did it ratchet up the heat and turn life into a semi-permanent hothouse for at least three full months of days slender and lean with light, summer shadows, full moons and dawns following sunsets with scarcely a break between, soothed by crickets, cuckoos and owls.

He continued to recite daily, with a little pushing from me of course. Last Sunday in June, for example, made it to Page 6 and then driven out to meet someone and, while waiting, I tickled his temporal and got him from 6 to 8 and one hour later, once he'd returned home, Page 8 to the end - staggered and disturbed but done.

C came up with an interesting idea for the framed pictures: up until then we'd envisioned them hung from the walls and the audience up close, a kind of open space where he could perform. She suggested, instead of mounting selected copies in frames on gallery walls, an easel was set up so each painting could be mounted as the story developed. It was an interesting idea but the 'canvasses' had to look like real paintings or as close as possible as anything that lacks authenticity stunts the ability to believe. That evening, about 9 pm and after an afternoon teaching English, we managed a good recital of the lines from very first to very last.

The search, meanwhile, went on for a venue in Angers that would take the show after Pont-Aven. A list obtained from the Town Hall as a guide, for two days he cycled around town looking at various spaces but finding the right one was only a small portion of the battle and it is a battle. By nature, people will always go with what they do know rather than what they don't know and under the hot, white sun of June, maintaining that philosophy was debilitating. We saw at least six spaces but couldn't just dive in and say: "Can you give me your space?" we first had to establish if it was the right size and then if it could be rented and not have to prove anything to anybody and do what he wanted.

With choosing the right paintings, the initial line of approach had been to go through the script and make a list of all the works mentioned, as well as characters that featured in my life and, if the characters that featured in my life were also painted by me, better still. It seemed logical to include only my paintings but how many people knew about Impressionism generally, to place 'me' in a context they could relate to? How much of the show had to explain the fundamentals of Impressionism and how the movement started and how much had to simply mention my place in it all? So Edgar Degas' 'Self Portrait', Georges Seurat's 'Sunday afternoon' and Louis Anquetin's 'Café de Clichy' suddenly seemed useful paintings to have in the set as they were contrasts from other Impressionist artists. Degas bought a lot of my work and kept me floating for many years, Seurat's

'Pointillism' – or The School of Dots as I unkindly referred to it – turned art into a science that made a painting look like a picture in a newspaper but I still had to appreciate the novelty. Anquetin turned up in Pont-Aven a few times, a big fan of Japanese stuff, and it showed.

Stowers' brain would suddenly go off at tangents and produce ideas but being tucked away in the folds of his grey matter, I could only glimpse their origins. Who are you onstage? Where are you in that context? What is this collection representative of: Tony's tastes or mine? Or is it simply a random trick? Thoughts and ideas constantly moving into shadow and then light, as we think we glimpse the final finished set and then doubt and see an alternative. Sometimes I could control what he thought and how he transformed his pictures and sometimes I couldn't. It was infuriating. It *is* infuriating!

An easel with fifteen mock canvasses would open up the freedom to choose non-art gallery venues and make the show open to just about any room anywhere capable of holding between 20 and 30 people. The downside was the images or the frames wouldn't stand up to close scrutiny. As framed images they'd be set at a distance from the audience to such a degree the outlines would be blurred.

"It's essential that I play in art galleries after Pont-Aven, P!"

I know that and you know that, but try telling people who think theatre is playing in a dark room with a stage at one end and everybody facing the same way sitting down - I had the same problems trying to get people to see art in a different way.

As each day went by and each new possibility entered, some instigated by me and some instigated against me, we tumbled between them all knowing that as we rolled, somewhere near the bottom the elements would come together and *together* we'd be able to make a joint decision to change from the imagined theory into the practical reality. Not having any spare budget for errors caused the stress.

I look into his memory banks to when he first arrived in France almost three years ago at the time of writing this, to his first weeks here: how he had hours rolling away in front of him, like a route-map waiting to be marked. Three years later he was neck-deep in the life - balancing trips to the dentists, teaching 30 irregular hours, having new hours added, visits to the photocopy shop to source images for Gauguin, shopping, teaching privately and spending hours at the computer sending out emails galore and co-ordinating rehearsals for the Shakespeare at the chateau – he'd created. But it was a job we both understood.

He wanted to recreate a short scene in Henry VI reproduced exactly as Shakespeare wrote it: set in front of the gate of the chateau and ramparts of Angers. The scene (Act 5, Scene 3) features the Earl of Suffolk, Margaret d'Anjou and her father King Rene - Suffolk negotiates marriage to Henry VI in return for peace across Anjou and Rene retaining his title. Shakespeare had written it as happening before the walls of the chateau of Angers so that probably meant one party on the road and the other party on the ramparts across the moat. Suffolk was English who probably spoke a smattering of bad French, which was why he was sent to negotiate. King René would have been the reverse: pure French with a smattering of bad English. Reduced down to a slow pace the language would have to be shouted almost word for word in order to be audible so this meant rather than performing an entire scene we just performed the minimum of lines.

T found two amateur French actors to shout exchanges across the 50' of space between the drawbridge and the ramparts but when T tried to communicate these developments to the director of the event he was first stonewalled for being too pushy and then banned from being involved! You see? People going with what they do know rather than what they don't – fear instead of curiosity.

As regards trying to find a space in Angers to perform Gauguin after Pont-Aven, he'd managed to get his hands on a list of possible venues: a shop that sold pictures but not really an art gallery, another that didn't exist at the address on the list, one – a room in a community centre near a language school was ideal but they didn't rent it and would only buy the show if they could see it - and unless they wanted to travel all the way to Pont-Aven, that was going to be difficult. Two other community centres: one big space, way too big - couldn't leave the set unattended - and the final space was only approachable by contacting by email. It was about then we started to think about more than just a flyer – we needed photographs, reviews, proof the show worked. That'd take months and we'd have to wait more months for possible performances.

"I couldn't wait. I had to be performing the show fresh from Pont-Aven in September – might as well have two for the price of one."

He returned to the Town Hall and through them met a collective of artists who hired a rough and ready old garage near the river. It looked promising and but the sole male of their group was an Alpha.

"I expect if I'd had long blonde hair and big tits, he'd have fallen over himself to help me."

So would I.

Finally, he was directed towards a tiny café/restaurant in the centre of the city - 20' x 20' – enough for maybe 15 chairs, some material to cover up the long mirror that filled one wall and re-arrange the furniture taking out the dining tables and replacing them again every night. There was no room to hang all the paintings for the four weeks he wanted the show to run, Thursday, Friday and Saturday night.

Why were you so obsessed with running the show for four weeks? It's unheard of!

"It's exactly *because* it's unheard of that I wanted to do it. Every performance would get better and people would have less excuse not to see it. I could maximise my earnings and offer something nobody else in town was offering."

He found a Salle des Fetes in Angers to hire but it was expensive. In Pont-Aven, if he lived there, the Salle Des Fetes would cost him nothing to hire but as he didn't, it was costing 85€ a day. That meant 9 people a day through the doors at 10€ each - just to pay the hire fee. In Angers, it was 85€ a day but seating was limited and only one show a day because few would want to see the show at any other time than the traditional 8.30 pm slot.

I had it easy by comparison – my work was done in days or weeks and then set on a wall and people wandered by day or night, not having to pay even a low entrance fee but being asked to pay ten or a hundred times that instead to walk away with the product. The images and words of a theatre play are no more than fading memories over cocktails, unlike the painting that was mounted and real. We went out and bought three frames for three of the photocopied images of my work: 'Mette Gauguin', 'Study of a nude: Suzanne sewing and 'The Vision' just to test how they looked. I have to say, through his eyes, they looked passable. I had a few pangs seeing Mette again. I remember that day when I painted her – the light in the room, the kids running in and out asking for things, Mette trying to keep them happy and stay still at the same time. We laughed a lot that day. But when later on I asked Suzanne the servant to strip off and pose, Mette went barmy. So, petulant child I sometimes was, I screwed Suzanne anyway when Mette was out and just as she plonked herself down on the edge of the bed with those little jubblies I said "Hold it there!" and the rest is history.

France is full of painters and art shops to cater for them. Ready-made canvasses are in most art shops - linen or cotton stretched over wooden frames. It would have been great to see the copied images stretched across real canvasses but almost impossible to achieve, as they'd have to be painted on as imitations and that would have to have been done by an expert and T couldn't afford an expert. It was frustrating not being able to operate hands and arms or I would have repainted them myself. He bought frames adequately sized to match the copied images but the 'Vision after the Sermon' needed a bigger frame because they weren't tailor-made to fit the size of the prints and he had to trim all the prints to get them to fit into the frames. In some cases this was okay but he had to cut off about 3 cm on the left and right sides of the 'Vision' and 2 cm off the top and bottom, to get it into the frame. On the one hand it reminded me the paintings were representatives needed to get the story moving along and didn't have to have exactly the same dimensions as the originals, but on the other I felt sick about his trimming them. It would have been like me cutting out opening lines from the starts and finishes of your plays.

"I welcome all input!"

Is that so, T? Well, did you consider this?

Whisper, whisper

"*You – you topped yourself at Hiva Oa?*"

Did I say that?

"Only three people saw you those last few days. Vernier gave you the last of the morphine, a storm cut off supplies. You tried to top yourself in '97 - Vincent and you talked about martyrdom and he'd done it. You were sinking fast. Have I missed something?"

Tioka!

I didn't need to say anymore and we never spoke about it again. The Eureka! seed was planted.

Meanwhile, he spent 100€ on the frames and about 30€ on copies. He still had an easel to buy, a comfy armchair to find and some clean carpet 6m x 4m to source, but 4m would never fit into his old Renault so it was time to kick around the idea of hiring a van to transport everything and, if needed, occasionally sleep in.

We caught a glimpse of the eventual costume in a French magazine in a dentist's waiting room: a pair of cool white trainers (or 'baskets' as they call them here), dark blue jeans, a white open-necked shirt and a loose and casual summer jacket. I have to say this wasn't my style: I loved outlandish outfits and liked to mix things up – clogs were great 'cause they lasted forever – but also double-breasted jackets with brass buttons and cravats or a safari hat.

"I'm *not* wearing fucking clogs, P!"

Instead, he wanted to dress me up like a peacock, an ass on the catwalk, a sideshow clown.

A few years ago in London when he performed Space Jockey, another Company was on the bill the same night as he performed and the young (and precocious) director had his cast learn all their lines but never did any blocking (the movements onstage). He just let them do their own blocking with each live performance. T had thought that was admirable and courageous and wanted to emulate it. Him being me was the nearest so far I got to actually *being* me again and I never quite understood the mindset of the actor until I moved into his head. With no director, he had to strive for a familiarity with the dialogue in a play with no fixed blocking.

As for getting to Pont-Aven and sustenance once there the easiest was to hire a van and in could go the 6m x 4m carpet, the armchair and easel (all yet to be bought) and the fifteen or so paintings, as well as luggage for one week, but this sort of thinking is theatre on a shoestring, theatre from the bottom end of the scale.

He was looking for a pleasant colour-combination for the set but unsure if the carpet should be blue or red or the armchair blue or red. The price of the carpet and availability of the colour would determine that, though I personally thought blue might be better for the carpet, as it'd also absorb the dust of feet.

About one hour's drive from Pont-Aven is the deep-in-Brittany home of his French friends Jacques and Sandrine and their daughter, Emily. Under the house they lived in (built on stilts of stone and fixed to the side of a hill) was a small studio. He'd already asked if they could either stay there for the duration of the shows or at least visit occasionally. There was a shower, so he saw no problem sleeping in the van near Pont-Aven alternate nights and then every other night driving back to their house and using the shower. C didn't like that idea very much and who could blame her - she spent half her working life in her car on the road between jobs and hated spending more time in vehicles than she had to. Instead, she opted for a hotel – if for some reason the run of shows didn't work out, at least they'd have a nice place to stay that'd cushion them through the worst.

T re-sent publicity out to a list of 12 destinations around Brittany responsible for promoting events through magazines and flyers, just to make sure they'd not forgotten the show the first time around.

Saturday 27th June 2009 finally saw Shakespeare on the battlements of the chateau of Angers. Despite a long period of hot weather, we sauntered up to the chateau to perform the *very* abridged snippet of 'Henry VI, Part 1', reproducing what even Shakespeare couldn't when writing the play in 1591. Then, about an hour before the agreed rendezvous at his flat in town, he received a call from the Chateau telling him they'd heard he was going to perform Shakespeare despite being told we couldn't. It was Shakespeare for God's sake! This was the first time it had ever been done - *ever*! Nonetheless, T couldn't be sure that they mightn't inform the local police or gendarmerie.

"The last thing I wanted – when just about to step forward from below the battlements and shout boldly up in a booming voice: "Do you speak English, your Majesty?" was a cop stepping in. I had visions of being led away in handcuffs, a martyr to the Shakespearian cause!"

The road in front of the battlements had been cleared of traffic so visitors could wander freely, so he hung around in the shade while C distributed flyers. The other actor F and the cameraman (DB) went into the chateau and took up positions on the battlements. With the help of the mobile phones we negotiated the start.

"René of Anjou, René of Anjou are – you – there?"

The transitional audience of background tourists suddenly stopped to watch as my voice boomed out. After the first performance, three local police on mountain bikes appeared, circled a couple of times and then left, so T sent 'Go!' again and performed again though this time medieval music from a local group nearby started up halfway through.

Then two cops on motorbikes arrived!

"It wasn't that I was worried about getting arrested – for the sake of the film we had to get through without interruption."

Luckily they too rode around and also disappeared and were no sooner out of the sight than he sent the third 'Go!' It was a job well done but he felt sure we hadn't heard the last of it.

Oh and he managed a nice read-through of his one-man show about me in the late evening of that same day but none at all on the Sunday.

Tuesday 30th June, we went out and bought the easel. It was a hot day, reducing everybody to traipsing around slowly from section-of-shade to section-of-shade. We first went to the Internet café and had a trawl for shops and eventually found a showroom on the old road to Paris and despite the heat of the day wandered very slowly along and finally found the shop we wanted. Two types of easel: 23€ and 42€. Trying to keep the budget down though not wishing to compromise on quality, he bought the cheapest and it was a relief to get it home, set it up and mount each of the three framed paintings onto it one by one. I felt a little charge when I took a peek through his eyes and saw my very own Mette languishing there on an easel. I remember the expanse of her white flesh, soft and yielding, and I became both nostalgic and horny but I'm not sure if ghosts can get horny.

Since early June he'd the idea he'd need carpet measuring 6m x 4m but it'd never fit into a transit van without being folded over and folded-over carpet looked naff. The other alternative was to cut two strips 6m x 2m but the 6m strip would be the long-ways strip, which would mean the join between the two pieces would be right down the middle of the floor space, probably passing under my chair and under the easel, more naff-ness. If he'd wanted to move around the carpet with any freedom, he'd need a one-piece, not two-piece but he become fixed on 6m x 4m because it'd fitted neatly into the rectangle between one corner of Salle Gauguin and a white pillar that joined the ceiling to the floor. So he measured out one, two and then three metres on the floor of his apartment and realised 3m x 3m would be much better - adequate to move around in and easier to get into or onto a car to transport. This suddenly meant we'd not need van hire and anyway van rental costs were more expensive than in England. Along with *kilometrage* (mileage) and fuel, it would have been a hefty bill to get the kit to Pont-Aven. The alternative was a roof rack, the easel, paintings, a comfy chair and suitcases for costumes and other clothes needed for the week that would all fit into or onto his car.

One Friday night I managed to persuade him to do the first four pages of his line-run walking from his flat to the cybercafé at about 9 and then, after the cybercafé, return home. But sleep got the better and body said "Bed!" and he was *almost* asleep when I gave the thalamus a good kick, he dragged himself out, propped up the script and read on until finally snoring. But he did it. With at least two line-run's we made real progress, the others mere memory-boosters. I understood 90% of what he said enough to know there were some sections he didn't understand at all. He'd learnt them from memory and knew that they *vaguely* meant what he *thought* they meant, so he re-read them and re-read them again and again until later on we managed a cracker of a read-through in the natural rhythm, a rushed 25-minute reading suddenly padding out to a 40-minute stroll. I was dead pleased. I put my feet up and watched the images roll past. An actor's life for me, T!

"A painter's life for me, P!"

9 - . . . and thickens . . .

Create your palette . . .

"Don't you want me to pose for you, Paul?"

No. Create your palette by using the colour wheel.Mix primary colours by -

"It seems easier to me if I posed for you, Paul."

I've got a memory haven't I? What do you think I am – a cabbage? Create your palette by using the colour wheel. Mix primary colours with a palette knife and make sure the colours are evenly blended and to make a shade . . .

"Until you came to Arles I'd no friends here. Nobody talked to me."

I wonder why, you daft twit. Mix in black. To make a tint, add white and -

'I can't work without models. I'm afraid of losing accuracy of form.'

To thin out paint use turps or to change its texture use sand or sawdust-

"But you give me courage to use my imagination, and it's true enough that paintings of this kind have something mysterious about them."

Impasto's will thicken the oil and prevent cracking

"I listen to you, you know? I listen to everything you say. You're a Godsend to me, Paul. I was so empty before you came. Don't overload your brushes, you said, cut out inessentials. I've tried, I'm trying!"

Set up your materials in a well-ventilated space

"I wish I could paint the nude as you do or the human figure even. Shall we go to the brothel again tonight, so as to study them?"

Prime the canvas with an application of white and apply paint direct from a tube or mixed with other oil.

"I'm so glad we're friends. I was afraid you only came to live with me because my brother was your dealer. Now I see I was mistaken. Your guidance has helped me so much. It would be so tragic if you were to leave just as we were producing some finer work."

Paint fat over lean

'Did I tell you how I admire Georges Seurat? He plans to form a kind of guild, as the builders of the Gothic cathedrals worked, to decorate public buildings and private houses with a series of large canvases or wall paintings. I know you don't think much of George and his "points".'

The School of Dots? Fuck that. Limit the palette to the basics: red, yellow, blue, brown, a black and a large tube of white. Mix secondary colours from these primaries.

"Painting a painting is like having a child isn't it? Is it like that? I can only imagine. It feels like giving birth!"

Sketch out your composition with a sable brush with basic shapes to use as guides. Contrast creates drama and by using close colours, harmony can be created. A colour's hue depends on red, blue or yellow. A painting should consist of 'warm' or 'cool' colours. Warm with yellow, rusty red or burnt orange, cools have blue and purple.

"I wish I had your luck with women, Paul. They part like Moses at the Red Sea when we go into the brothels, but what about your wife and children in Copenhagen? You talked about an exhibition in Brussels – do you think that's wise? Brussels and Copenhagen are a stone's throw apart. Your wife might get her claws into you again and take you away from me. And then what would I do? Where would I be? Alone again!"

I'm not surprised you're alone – you're fucking insane! And you're impotent, as impotent as a castrated goat! Women don't touch you because you don't try to inspire desire - you try to inspire pity! You stink, your teeth are yellow, broken and rotting, your face is cracked and filthy with paint, you never shave and dress like a tramp! This hero worship makes me sick! "Where would I be? Alone again!" And you – what do you inspire? You gad about with the scum of this Godforsaken town in every stinking café. Only the dregs flock to you because it takes dregs to know dregs! The wasters, the spongers, full of self-pity! Oh yes, you love my paintings, but when I've done them you always find something wrong! I've spent hours and hours listening to your talk of the Master of this and the Master of that – where's there influence in your work? You talk and talk and talk but you do nothing!

"We're like martyrs you and I, aren't we, Paul? Martyrs for our art, ha! If it came down to a choice on how to go, what would you choose? A rope? Poison? Drowning?"

"Do you know what your brother said to me about you, Vincent? Do you?"

"No, Paul, what did he say?"

'There's something about Vincent' he said, "Something in the very way he speaks that forces people either to like or dislike him - violently. He can't be indifferent - it's love or hate all the time. He spares no one's feelings.'

There are tears in his eyes but I can't help myself, the anger boils over, weak people were put on this earth for the pleasure of the strong. God forgive me, forgive me. Instead I lower my voice and calmly say: "So make coffee, roll a cigarette and shut your fucking mouth!"

* * *

Early July I received a phone call from the company that rented out the rehearsal space: they'd cancelled the contract for the rehearsal room from 1st – 8th August. The City Council owned the rehearsal space and word had got out that I'd performed at the chateau despite being banned and so I was to be punished for performing, despite its success.

C offered her empty barn so, one barn door closes, another barn door opens. DB, the cameraman, whom I'd first met when he'd filmed the English Workshop for under-privileged children Christmas 2006 *and* who'd also helped with Shopping with Shakespeare 4, finished the film of Shakespeare at the Chateau on 27th June. It came in at just under four minutes. We'd done three runs in all and he'd filmed two from the battlements and one from the road. The second was interrupted by medieval music but he did a sterling job and 'Shopping with Shakespeare 5' was added to You Tube where it still rests today.

Then I went to find the carpet for Pont-Aven. Needless to say I shouldn't have arrived at lunchtime. So, once the workers at the carpet shop had finished eating, I spent 83€ on a lovely piece of fresh, clean 3m x 3m turquoise shag that *just* fitted into the length of my car, rolled up correctly and a few cm trimmed off one end.

I also popped into a cloth shop and bought a 2m x 1m piece of red cotton to drape over the easel and then went to speak to the owner of the tiny café about Gauguin, thinking of performing in the same weekend as 'Les Accroches Coeur', a big outdoor theatre festival from 11th – 13th September, hoping to skim off visitors for Gauguin. Les Accroches Coeur was a perfect opportunity to stimulate an 'off', as the French call fringe theatre.

I popped in to the Town Hall to see about adding Shakespeare to the Festival but rather than see our small effort as part of the rich tapestry of life, they scolded me, telling me they found my attitude unprofessional and 'forbade' me from doing anything for the Festival. I asked if they intended to continue to challenge my spirit of self-expression. No reply.

C had had a party at her house in mid-July and the big barn had been completely swept and cleaned up in anticipation of bad weather. Luckily the weather held and the party went ahead so the barn was still empty and beckoning to be filled and as it was only two weeks before Pont-Aven, I made use of it, though I still had to buy some lamps and get the programmes – 100 in English, 100 in French - and do some wardrobe shopping. At last, after months, I'd a clear view and could count down the days.

I popped in by chance (and on the spur of the moment) to a small theatre space near my flat in Angers called La Comédie and showed them my Pont-Aven publicity. It wasn't a great space but better than a tiny back room in a café and they were generous enough to offer a 50/50 split on box office, which was the best offer yet. I agreed to contact them after the holidays of mid-July and mid-August.

My thoughts were turning to what I could cook up on a shoestring budget for Les Accroches Coeur on the 11th, 12th or

13th September. What I needed most was a performance space or a flat with a first floor balcony would be ideal as a platform with one actor on the balcony, another down on the street in amongst the crowd? The grey matter ticked.

On Saturday 25th July, I finally got the set for Gauguin together in the barn, being rigorous, preserving everything in the best condition, spending ten minutes sweeping the workshop floor, checking electricity and laying out newspaper and gradually unrolling the carpet over it. The easel fitted squarely onto the carpet and then the big Spanish chair alongside.

The Spanish chair had been stumbled on. In my imagination I'd thought it'd be modern, in keeping with the costume and that rainbow effect in the set. Everything had to work together – props, costume, set and colours. I'd always thought of the set as having to be symbolic and the easel to be draped with a red cloth, to represent the lifeblood of the artist.

"Or the colour Emile Bernard saw when he first saw 'The Vision' after he'd shown me 'Breton Girls in a Meadow'! He accused me of plagiarism!"

The blue carpet would represent the sea on which Gauguin had spent his early days and because water was the main transport of men and materials in those days, all his intercontinental travel had been done by land or by sea around the world, to Peru, to Tahiti, to Panama, and all featured in his paintings.

"Or the fact that the only other cheap carpet in the shop was black or orange!"

I was torn between yellow or green for a chair, yellow representing fear and mortality and green representing the greenery of the nature that featured in his work.

"Yellow represented the chicken-shits who outnumbered me at Concarneau and green the colour of my puke after a bottle of absinthe,"

But, as it happened, my friend C said: "What about this?" and we found, in the darkness of the unlit barn, a squat and solid, straight-backed wooden chair fit for a Celtic King with a hand-sewn leather seat and back and carved legs. And it was heavy. I laboured it down the steps and across to the house and carefully washed off the dust and gave the upholstery a waxing and voila - another piece of the jigsaw was in place.

"Peru! I'd spent at least the first four years of my life in Peru as a child because my parents took refuge there with relatives. I passed a lot of time carving wood as well as painting."

I ran through the show three times on Sunday and twice on Saturday. What a difference it made, the diverse elements that for so long had been in my imagination coming together! It was a beautiful weekend too with a 35C sun crawling slowly up to its apex in a sky unblemished by clouds, a shaft of sunlight falling through the broken windows of the barn with slowly shifting dust patterns.

Amongst a stack of old broom handles I found a crutch and tried to use it as Gauguin had used one after being booted in the leg at Concarneau. It *seemed* to work but I knew immediately I wouldn't use it in the run-through.

"Are you trying to recreate me or are you Tony Stowers possessed of me?"

I unloaded the framed paintings from their suitcase with tender care and needed to find a way to store the fifteen frames on set and refer to each as I arrived at specific points in the script. I didn't want to lean them against the back wall of the room in Pont-Aven as that would have meant stating the wall existed and if the wall existed then the room existed and if the room existed, the building existed and if the building existed then this wasn't an attempt by an actor to transport his audience into an other world, but an acknowledgement that the real world existed. Such was my odd logic, but then again, not so odd. I started by stacking all the paintings on one side of the chair and then shifted them one-by-one to the easel when each was needed, trying to find the balance with that movement so it didn't look robotic. The routine, for example, was: mention the painter or character = pick up the required image = pop it into the easel. To keep the spontaneity, I gave the impression the images provoked the spontaneity of the words and not the other way round. There was a temptation to put all of them onto the easel one after the other, but I managed to keep one on my lap on the chair, the portrait of my dead daughter Aline.

"Children shouldn't die before their parents - it upsets the natural order of things."

How would I separate the voices of certain characters in Gauguin's life, especially his estranged wife Mette and Edgar Degas? When I saw the paintings of Mette and the self-portrait of Degas in their frames on set, it was suddenly obvious: reproduce the physical positions posed in for the paintings, that way the audience is able to make the link. I was aware too of the approaching challenge of filling that big empty space at Pont-Aven with crisp, articulate, controlled, spoken language. Reciting to an empty space is easy but the real challenge is facing the audience members when they're staring intently. The lighting wasn't bright enough to make them invisible to me. This wasn't a good thing. It meant I'd be at the mercy of individual reactions and unconsciously try to please one face instead of all. Some would laugh, some wouldn't. Twice in run-throughs without an audience I lost my way, entertaining long pauses as I re-sought the path again or repeated the most recent line in an effort to remember. This latter course (repeating the same line) is best, as it appears the character is simply underlining a point in repeating it - when the truth is the actors has probably forgotten what comes next! What was really missing? An audience, of course! I'd been going over these lines day after day for almost four months – that's over 100 – with no audience. I was as lonely as Van Gogh!

"Ah Vincent – don't start me on that one!"

I can't say my effort to get in-shape for the show worked. I'd been on a diet for two months but despite losing 5 kilos very early on, seemed to have stabilised at 85. I should have done some exercise but didn't but was at least happy that I wasn't smoking though after seven months off I still coughed up gunge every few days or so. I couldn't say I was out of the woods neither – often in the company of smokers I continued to feel the pull, though it was less strong once the immediate addiction was broken. My teeth and smile had improved hugely given all the time (and money) spent in the French dentist's chair: two new crowns and a major frontal polish to get rid of accumulated stains. I'd suddenly got a fantastic smile again of which I was unashamed and it meant nothing could hold me back from using a full range of emotions and facial features not only in the show but also in close-contact situations as a teacher.

A French friend, F, came over one afternoon and in the sunny garden we translated the programme for Pont-Aven. There was about two hours work all told though and I was grateful for their work and effort. Our friends and family are unsung heroes.

"You can say that again, T – without a long-suffering wife, generous friends and my Uncle Isidore's bequest, I'd have been out on the streets with a tin cup."

I decided to hold a private performance on Saturday 8th August in the barn so set about inviting a quite few people but very few responded, it was after all the time when most people were away on holiday. Monday morning I gave an interview to Virgin Radio in Angers about Gauguin and I also went on to the Internet to see if the show was being listed anywhere and was relieved to see a few circulars appearing around Quimper, Finisterre and south Brittany.

Meanwhile, I still needed two lamps. I'd thought maybe one orange and one green bulb. All the picture frames had glass fronts and once set on the easel were pointing up at a slight angle. The audience of course was sitting so any lights in the ceiling would bounce off the glass. The lamps, I imagined, would be set at ground level, shining upwards, giving a kind of spooky look.

In early July I'd written to a small, private French theatre in Paris and asked if they'd be interested in booking my show. A fortnight later, just as I was about to set off to Pont-Aven, they replied asking if would be interested performing there in mid-September? The drawback was that I'd have to hire the space for 170€ but Paris had to be better than Pont-Aven in terms of reviews – reviews meant more bookings. Email news from Pont-Aven meanwhile was that the poster and flyer distribution had started and would continue right up until the 11th August.

On the 1st August 2009 I finally came to grips with the fact THE month had arrived when I was able to count down the days - but still so much to do!

We (Paul and I) went out shopping to buy some spanking new jeans and three white shirts for the show - that was easy - then I had to buy something to illuminate the stage - not so easy.

I spent about 20 minutes in the Lighting Department of the local hypermarket, having found some simple angle-poises with round half-globe heads that could be swivelled and I had three in my hands and was walking towards the cash register when I calculated: each bulb was 40 watts, multiplied by three = 120 watts - about enough to illuminate a living room from the ceiling down but nowhere near strong enough to cast a bathing light over all the props or illuminate the face of the actor. I wrestled with this for minutes and then suddenly dumped them on the nearest shelf and left - there had to be a better solution. I'd noticed a display of Halogen lamps but they didn't appear to have mains leads and mains leads were needed so whoever operated lights would be able to control the on/off positions from a distance. Halogens can be blinding, so without something to control their intensity I was going to be blinded. As chance would have it, on the drive back to C's house after the aborted supermarket trip, in a little village called Chavagnes-les-Eaux, I drove past a building that belonged to David the Clown and pulled up outside.

David the Clown was known locally simply as 'Le Clown' on account of how, for 25 years, that had been his profession. He'd performed for parties, kids and schools all over France but in recent months he'd retired and gone into antiques, reshaping his former Clown School into a display space fit for a *brocante*, as the French call antiques dealers. I figured if Le Clown had recently been in the business he might have some equipment I could use and if not he might at least know somebody who did? And there it was, tucked away at the back: a mixing desk and a Halogen atop a three-legged scaffold pole. I offered to rent it for the period I'd be in Pont-Aven and invited David to C's barn a few days later to install it. Seeing the mixing desk had room for up to six lights, I realised there was nothing stopping me going back to the same hypermarket as before and buying two Halogens as a mixing desk would allow the intensity to be controlled and reduced.

Meanwhile, thoughts drifted back to Les Accroches Coeur, the theatre festival planned for Angers in September. Angers in recent years has had, along with many other French cities, problems with immigrants, the generally displaced or homeless, *sans papers* is what they're termed, 'without papers', identity cards, passports or work visas. They sometimes move from squat to squat where they can at least live under a roof with clean running water whilst going through various legal processes to stay in France. Such a building was in the newspaper in Angers in early August: a former hairdressing salon had been occupied by an efficient team of *sans-papiers* and hit the headlines because the building was in the centre of town – an eyesore for the tourists.

What about a bilingual crossover of Shakespeare's Julius Caesar, the scene when Brutus and Mark Antony mourn the recently assassinated Caesar except I substitute the word 'Caesar' for the word 'justice', asking why 'French justice' should only apply to French people and not to oppressed people from around the world? I also found Jean-Jacques Rousseau the legendary French philosopher's quote: *"The first man who, having fenced in a piece of land, said 'This is mine,' and found people naive enough to believe him, that man was the true founder of civil society. From how many crimes, wars, and murders, from how many horrors and misfortunes might not any one have saved mankind, by pulling up the stakes, or filling up the ditch, and crying to his fellows: Beware of listening to this impostor; you are undone if you once forget that the fruits of the earth belong to us all, and the earth itself to nobody"* to add on. With the new Halogens, two actors and good use of height and shadow, as well as some sampled AC/DC (Hell's Bells) and the first floor balcony of the squat, I'd make a little scene to highlight the problems of the *sans-papier*. But in the end, however, I couldn't get it co-ordinated and felt the squatters had more important problems on their hands, so despite my imagination running away, the idea fizzled out shortly afterwards*.

I drove to the big French DIY store Leroy Merlin, took the plunge and bought two new 500W Halogens and some duct tape and then drove over to the barn. Later on, once the lamps had been loaded with bulbs, David came over and we set them up around the base. The illumination was incredible! It looked great but we also needed an overhead to balance the light and it had to be central: two sides were well lit, stage left and stage right, but there was a grey area between so early next day David returned with the upright telescopic pole.

Very late that night, after 10, by which time the hot sun had set and plunged the workshop into a darkness interrupted only by fluttering bats, I ran the show again with these new lights for the benefit of two guests. I was apprehensive as it was the first time I'd run everything together in a co-ordinated way and it was no great or memorable performance. But it worked.

Saturday night was the first run-through with tech and dress. I was relaxed. When I cast my mind back to past occasions when I'd a tech run or dress run before going public, I was often a bag of nerves but of course that was more often than not artificially-induced - too much coffee and cigarettes - but if you're prepared there's no need to be nervous.

I was due to start at 7 pm but one of the invitees was late so I didn't actually kick in until 8 pm. I'd initially thought C would operate a more complicated lighting plan in which she'd jump from light to light as I moved around the stage but as she'd have a dual role at Pont-Aven - operating the lights and fielding the door – I advised her not to, to be able to concentrate on my words with no distractions.

I found myself looking into the eyes of individual audience members as I'd expected. I found myself reading expressions and trying to change the negative expressions to positive ones. My desire to be completely free in expression was limited by the poor lighting. But the show went fine otherwise, the only criticism from my audience being on the odd occasions when I introduced a painting, the lights reflected in the glass. The other criticism was some French mispronunciations and that I should allow the Doctor (who diagnosed Gauguin with syphilis) to stay in silence for a little longer before delivering his bad news.

As it was my birthday the day after we all got a bit drunk afterwards and danced, C's imitation of Bjork's 'It's oh so quiet' being the crowning glory.

The following day I returned to Angers, packed my suitcase, gathered up tools I thought maybe useful, took a CD player and then it was back to the barn to pack the car.

When I cast my mind back to that first crazy idea in 2007 and then 2008 of performing in Pont-Aven, it seemed hard to imagine I was finally on the threshold in 2009. After over a hundred years, Gauguin's ghost was going back to Pont-Aven to be with the spirits of dead friends.

"Everything we do we should do for ourselves because it feels right. Hard to believe it'd been over 18 months since I'd first set eyes on you in Pont-Aven that January day in 2008, T."

Eighteen months later, I was ready. What lay ahead? Would anybody come? Would I recover my outlay or make a loss? I didn't know, but that wasn't the reason I'd set out to do all this in the first place - I did it first for myself and second for Gauguin.

"And I won't forget that, Mr Stowers, I won't forget that."

* The Welsh pub in Angers on 11th and 12th September '09 with F and myself in an adapted version (Shopping with Shakespeare 6) of Richard III. I hated it.

10 - . . . until finally . . .

When the weather's good, people go out but when the weather's bad, they lounge about getting restless and bad-tempered. So it is with artists - just about every portrait you've ever seen was probably painted when it was pissing down outside. That's how I ended up with Mam'selle Satre. She agreed to sit in her typical Breton dress while outside a year's supply of rain fell in one day, gurgling down the roofs and gutters and pouring into rain barrels that overflowed and gushed into street.

Very proud she was - nobody had ever asked her to sit for a painting. She'd a local beau and a couple of brothers - burly, ignorant types with faces like leather who disliked us, mocked our clothes and accents or made jokes about our white hands and unworked bodies. They didn't often do it to our faces but there's was a hard world all year round of toil and labour in winter and summer, fishing and drowning on dangerous seas, or early deaths under blankets of damp weather and snow. We didn't suffer the world of the other: to them we were coddled and though neither me nor many of my friends were in reality very wealthy, for the villagers anybody who could afford to take six months of the year off to paint pictures was either stupid or unnecessarily rich and since even they knew stupidity didn't guarantee wealth, they presumed the latter. But they liked our money. Oh how they liked our money. It bought them things they would otherwise never have imagined buying. But they didn't display their profits extravagantly because that would have offended their austere manners and customs. We brought in money to the pensions and the hotels yes, but in other ways too – we bought paints and brushes in stores owned by local people, we spent copiously in the inns and bars, bought breads and cheeses, spent fares on carriages and bought tobacco and candles, postage stamps and newspapers or spent handsomely on the village doctor. This was money that, were it not for painting and painters, would never have found its way into their pockets. When I offered to paint Madame Angèle Satre she blushed in that way women do. From the other villagers one sensed, mingled with envy, a certain mistrust.

Needless to say, her knowledge of painting was firmly in the "traditional" – if she didn't look like a Greek goddess, I'd failed. She had a family and parents to take care of so she could only give me an hour or so a day over the course of a week of rain. She consistently asked to see the work over the hours I worked on it but I said no. In retrospect, perhaps I should have said yes, that way she could have prepared herself and come to understand something of the delicacy of the process but her natural curiosity rose and her imagination ran wild. I'd shown it to some friends at my pension to ask what they though beforehand but reactions were mixed and some male friends of her family accused me of ridiculing her. One of them offered to destroy it for me to save her the pain and when I refused, offered to knock my block off. Madame Gloanec calmed the situation, but only for a short while. Soon after, Madame Satre got to hear the wildly exaggerated news and demanded to see it and what she saw in the end could never ever have matched what she'd expected.

"I've two red cheeks and a red nose, Mr Gauguin. And what's that heathen idol doing in the picture? I'm a God-fearing Christian. What flowers are those? We don't have such flowers in this part of the world! And the title – Beautiful Angela! What a horror!"

I forget my response, something like: "What did you expect? I'm not a cartoonist who flatters his subjects so they look nice for the neighbours."

"I never want to see you or that painting again as long as I live, Mister Gauguin!"

It hadn't been the first time – the year before I'd offered "The Vision" to the church in the village and the priest, more concerned with what his simple-minded parishioners would think than what he thought, refused it, as did the church at Tremalo. Nobody gave a toss about my work in Pont-Aven. They only ever wanted to appear respectable to each other and skim money off us, glad to see the back of us at winter so their consciences could return to their usual narrow frames. They wanted to be told what was good for them by the Pope and his Bishops in distant Rome, not by penniless drunks. There was a primitive rage simmering beneath the surface and they were often just itching to wade in and tear us apart. In Concarneau, it finally came to the surface.

* * *

We drove up on the Monday morning and arrived around lunchtime to a small town milling with tourists and kids though Pont-Aven was hardly a place to bring kids – there was nothing for them to do apart from eat ice cream and moan. The three spindly roads in and out of the town were nose-to-tail with cars, camper vans and caravans. As soon as we arrived we saw copies of the poster everywhere as we chugged slowly towards the centre. The centre is pretty much built around Place Gauguin, the Town Hall, Salle Gauguin, the public toilets, two bars, the tourism office and a couple of galleries and shops that sell biscuits.

Beyond that, a chunky bridge crosses the bubbling River Aven, on the other side a clutch of cafes and shops and then galleries stretch down to the harbour side (where our hotel was and boats moored in the tidal river) or up and out to the south and west lined with more galleries, a bank, a chemist's and so on. Everything can be traversed on foot in less than five minutes but when it's full of tourists and traffic takes longer and there were hundreds of people who didn't seem to know where to go or what to do, apart from traipse from shop to shop and bar to bar drinking beers and coffees and eating ice cream. Surely we could find a paltry 9 people a day to come and see the show? That's all we needed for the hire fee, more than that would go towards paying for the poster distribution.

We went to the Town Hall, picked up the keys and I unloaded the car and set while C went to get us installed in the hotel. The floor swept, I sussed out where the white screens were and fixed them up. A lot of tourists seemed to be stopping outside the door - but only to look at the two hand-painted maps of Pont-Aven mounted each side of the entrance. I stayed positive.

As I unrolled the carpet and set up the lights I realised it was noisy outside! I'd been there five times that year already and it had been dead. But there just *had to be* a few people that'd show a passing interest in a theatre show that only lasted 40 minutes about the life of a man whose name and work was everywhere.

I placed 27 chairs around the performance space, got the lights working, set aside a corner to get changed when people arrived, gathered together as many of the A3 posters (haphazardly pinned up around the place with no real consideration by Town Hall staff) as I could find and taped them up in the front windows - in particular removing one posted insalubriously under the word TOILETS - and found a billboard and made a display. Looking back, it'd have been smart to shoot photos on the Monday and spend time on Photoshop and then Tuesday could have driven to the larger town of Concarneau (more sophisticated photocopy shops) and printed up photos and put these around the outer edge of the billboard so anybody vaguely interested could have looked and maybe been half-persuaded. For strangers to be persuaded, they usually need reassurance from somebody else their money won't be wasted and I had no reviews. Not that this stopped them from frittering it on biscuits, postcards and beer, but of course they could, from past experience, qualify those things - a new theatre show wasn't easy to qualify. What held me back from extra promotion was how much money I'd already spent and part of me thought: "I don't need to spend any more money on yet another wing and a prayer – there'll be enough here to get 9 people a day in." I'd overheads and money going out of my bank account in August on rent, distribution of publicity, an unpaid dentist bill and an MOT (*contrôle technique* or CT the French call it) on my car but I had to keep reminding myself I wasn't in Pont-Aven to make millions, just to say that the show played Pont-Aven first and enjoy a well-earned holiday. It was a way to break in the show because I knew that the performance I'd done the previous Saturday was nowhere near the quality of what I *could* and *should be* delivering.

My main memory that first day was the tourists who left very little space in which any memory of the Impressionist painters that haunted this quiet valley around the end of the 19th century could dwell or still be found. The little River Aven spilled down from the Black Mountains in middle Brittany, though they were hardly mountains, hills really. Huge granite boulders the size of small cars were scattered around the valley, as indeed they've been scattered round half of Brittany. Residents of the valley had, over the centuries, channelled the sides of the river in order to increase the speed of the flow and then around this built their water mills – the town is full of their traces. There's a short series of walkways and bridges around the back of the main square and street on footbridges that show the old steps that led from back gardens down to the river where nineteenth century Breton laundry women spent their lives washing clothes or catching the trout that teem in the river in the summer months. When I'd been there back in January I could've tasted and almost touched the authenticity of Pont-Aven as those Impressionist painters had seen it, even though most of them came in the summer months. But the day I was finally there in summer 2009 it had atrocious traffic, over-priced restaurants and bars and absolutely zero going on after 7 pm.

The British tourists didn't help. I think it's connected to their inability to adapt. However, in Pont-Aven we needed their money and so at 1.30 pm on that first day I diligently dressed in my spanking new costume of white shirt, black jeans and trainers and waited.

And waited.

2 pm came.

And went.

C looked more depressed than me. I was *slightly* pissed off, despite the fact my publicity was everywhere but I'd been steeling myself psychologically, having experienced it before. Nonetheless, I had to accept that two o'clock in the afternoon wasn't the best time of day to get people to see a show, so we returned to the hotel.

About an hour later an old friend from Angers turned up and went away again, promising to return for the 8.30 show. We returned to Salle Gauguin at 4.30.

I dressed again.

And waited.

And waited.

By ten past five nobody had come, yet again, and yet again despite the fact that the town was teeming with tourists. No, I tell a lie: one man showed up late but we were on our way back to the hotel so we asked if he'd be kind enough to come back in the evening for the 8.30. The evening show would be more enticing as it was the end of the day and there wasn't much to do around those parts, so why not see a show? If I didn't get 9 people in, 6 would do and maybe I'd recoup the loss later in the week?

By 8.40 pm only my friend from Angers had returned and the local man and only he paid. I was 80€ out of pocket at the end of my first day.

The performance was difficult. I'd forgotten to dim the lights at the back of the room so was treated to seeing C moving around behind the two-headed audience. Then my Angers friend started filming me on his video camera and moving round the room at the same time – he hadn't told me and I hadn't expected it. It was a poor show, out of focus, perfunctory and wandering, like a glorified rehearsal. It's a strange feeling: body moving robotically, the words constantly cued up in the memory and delivered from brain to mouth. But another voice keeps breaking in from time to time: "Why hasn't she switched the lights off?" or "How can I make a sign to her to get her to do that?" or "Why is he filming? Doesn't he appreciate how difficult this is?"

The following day – Wednesday – we decided not to bother turning up for the 2 pm performance and in the afternoon drove over to a small seaside town called Le Pouldu. It was here in 1889 that Gauguin visited a Dutch painter friend called Jacob Meyer de Haan and stayed in a kind of B&B called 'Buvette de la Plage', run by a single woman called Marie Henry. She was from Brittany originally but, having saved a small amount of cash working as a house servant in Paris for ten years, had returned to open up her own B&B. It was at her hotel that some Impressionist painters contributed to the decoration of the downstairs rooms by painting directly onto the walls, windows and doors. The hotel had since been restored to its original standard and the paintings re-copied as the original painted panels had been taken or bought by Americans in the 1930's. It was worth the visit, a welcome relief from Pont-Aven where few of Gauguin's old haunts are preserved in their original state. I think we sensed old friends that day.

Gauguin was lucky in the respect that he was able to exchange his paintings for a bed and food at Pension Gloanec in Pont-Aven. I couldn't see the local Town Hall exchanging free performances of my show for our hotel accommodation or rental fee. C had said in early June I wasn't welcome in Pont-Aven: they didn't want some foreigner coming in and blowing away the myth of the 'gentleman rogue'. I'd read Gauguin was somebody you either loved or hated, where his outlandish clothes and behaviour (which to him and me was original, brave and daring) was, to these provincial locals, provocative, ridiculous and mocking. Or was I just being paranoid?

We turned up for the 5 pm show but nobody came.

To break the ice, C took up the script and went through an impersonation of me doing the show. It was funny and light and helped me chill out and we used the opportunity to take lots of photos, though it took two shoots to get the best. That evening the only visitor was a journalist from the local newspaper.

And finally, it happened – the best performance ever (so far) . . .

"C'était politique, mais je n'étais pas aveugle !"

11 - Gauguin's Ghost

The ocean oh the ocean! The things these eyes have seen, the places, the people! Why? What was it all for eh? I learned to cook, to drink, to whore, to think, to fight, to fight, whoa how I fought . . . six years in the Navy, stoking the boilers mind you, not poncing it as Petty Officer in white shirt with gold-braid, and I found nowt on land that replaced the freedom of the sea, nowt, not even painting, swear down! So, Monsieur Gauguin, tell us about your life.

I thought you'd never ask, pet. Me life I lived as I chose: I said please and thank you, bowed for ladies, shook hands with men, kept my dignity, shared what little I had. But it wasn't enough. Why? Because I know what you say about us: you say: "Gauguin? Isn't he the one who dumped his wife and kids to go off to Tahiti and shag them lasses in hula hoop skirts? Well, it wasn't *quite* like that but then nothing ever is, is it?

Rewind time: a hundred and forty, fifty, sixty years ago? Peru, I remember Peru. 1848, the French *coup d'état,* Napoleon III, just after . . . Mam and Dad ran . . . I was *this* big (he indicates the height of a small child) . . . relatives there, Peru . . . *en route* my

Dad's heart (he indicates an explosion of his chest) . . . in Peru, me Uncle Don Pio took us to a bullfight for me seventh birthday . . . gives us a bull's ear as a trophy . . . ah, the passion of South America . . . four years in exile and when I got back to France, an accent like a Peruvian donkey! Bishop Dupanloup, high school in Orleans: "So, young Eugene Henri, tell me: what do you want to be when you grow up?" I'd settle for being a living legend, Father Dupanloup. "A living legend? Did you hear that, Lord? Eugene Henri, half of you is tame and half of you, wild. I blame your childhood. Peruvians are savages: cannibalism, human sacrifice and idol worship. This is France, not Peru. Here we write the rules of civilization, there they test them. How can you hope to get good qualifications without French, all day long drawing and sketching and no father of your own to whip you into shape? What's that, Lord? Yes, I think you're right. You must go on studying your Bible – you're at least good at that - but I must give you two with the stick for audacity!"

When me Mam died I wasn't too sad 'cause her spirit of independence passed into me, but independence is nothing without contacts. Enter Uncle Gustave. An 'uncle' is what you call your Mam's bit-on-the-side when your real Dad fucks off.

"Before your mother died, Paul, I promised, as your guardian, to take care of you, so I've found you a job. You are to start at Bertin's as a *liquidateur*. Outside of the Official Stock Exchange is a second group of traders called *coulissiers*. They stabilize share prices, which is a good thing for countries like ours wrecked by the Prussians, trying to rebuild Paris. You settle up the dealings between the *coulissiers* and the shareholders on time and in full. "Am I qualified for such a job, Uncle?" you ask. Six years at sea *and* you saw action? You've broad shoulders. You'll need them - sound credentials for the art of persuasion. It's well paid – mostly commission - and dull as ditchwater. But don't fret - all my life I worked dull, stupid jobs as a means to an end. You can start Monday. Meanwhile, some new paintings have arrived. Art and culture in this day and age is revolution Paul - buying it is the act of a subversive. I must do something with my money and art excites, as I'm too old to man barricades or plant black flags. Camille Pissarro, a Jew, is coming for tea with his friend Claude Monet. A new style of painting's emerging, did you know? We shall have to think of a name for this new style for it's leaving an impression," and then I was blessed by the hands of the Impressionists - a name foisted on them by a Parisian reviewer: Monet, Manet, Cezanne, Sisley,

Renoir, and Degas. The approval of Degas meant the most. He taught us about the use of memory.

"Marvellous" he goes, "we invite you to exhibit a *painting* in the Fourth Impressionist Exhibition and you submit a piece of *sculpture*. Gauguin, you're determined to stand out. I admire that. But be careful – don't push your luck, not with me, for I despise the term "Impressionism" and I hate gangs. In fact, I hate gangs almost as much as I hate Jews." "Aw hey," I says, "that's not very PC that, Edgar mate! My teacher Pissarro says you're a bastard in some ways but frank and loyal in others. "Pissarro?" he goes. "Don't presume 'cause a man likes your work, he also likes you, Gauguin." "I'll make a note of that the next time you show interest in one of me works, Monsieur Degas," I says, dead tongue-in-cheek, like you know? "Look Gauguin," he goes, "It's all very well to copy what one sees, but it's much better to draw what one remembers. Imagination links with memory. Reproduce only what's striking, which is to say only what's necessary. Thus, your memories and fantasies are liberated from the tyranny of Nature."

Wise words. He snubbed me many times in the beginning did Degas. He wasn't the only one: many people snubbed me, not only 'cause I was stubborn but also 'cause I was untrained. True, I was isolated and lonely but I produced, I did produce. I was very productive and very reproductive: my long-suffering wife, Mette. They say many men often marry their Mothers but in my case I seem to have married me Grandmother.

Having said that, my real Granny was Flora Tristan - 'The Worker's Saint' - a radical feminist and socialist beacon, but I married a Danish pastry: Mette Gad from Copenhagen. All she wanted was a rich husband and an account at the best pie shop in town. Instead she got five kids and me . . .

"I don't understand, dear husband, why must we move to a poorer part of Paris? I'm happy here. And why do we rarely go to the theatre or the opera? You spend all your spare time painting or mixing with your artist friends in cafes and restaurants. I never see you. I gave up the dullness of Copenhagen for life with you in gay Paris, but not this life. What about our children?"

And there was me in my own world: "Whose work to see next and why: so I can learn from them, the Masters. They'd trained at the Academy. Who else can teach me but them?" "What did I just say, Paul?" she'd say. "I don't know pet, too wrapped up in my own world with thoughts of which painting to submit to the exhibition at the Salon in 1876. I thought maybe 'The Seine at the Pont D'Iena'. What do you think?"

I queued for hours in a line that stretched around four buildings and then we all passed in front of the judges like railway carriages in a station. They sky-ed me, up near the ceiling, but it was a start. "Copied straight from the style of Corot," they said. That's what pleased the judges from The Salon – bunch of old wankers. It's not a question of copying. It's a question of experiencing as much as you can and from that vast array identifying the missing link. That missing link becomes your own style, the next generation.

And as for marriage: *Mette - left – me*, I didn't leave Mette. In '79 I made 30,000 francs from the Market! We were rolling in it, man! How couldn't she have been happy with that? Oh she *was* happy, so happy she spent it as fast as I made it. Okay, it wasn't exactly like *that:* in '84 we went to Copenhagen and I organised an exhibition of me work, but after five days it was closed down by the fucking Danish Academy. "Fuck off!" they said. "I want to go back to Paris", I tell the wife. "Fuck off then!" she said. "Fuck off!" said her family. *That* was the start of my painful, painful apprenticeship. "It's not my problem!" that's the slogan these days.

In '81, I met Cezanne.

"What did you mean, Monsieur Cezanne, when you said you thought Impressionism was smouldering and some new form was being created from its ashes?" I ask him. "I cannot stop you looking at my work, Gauguin, but you'll not have the key to my soul!" he replies. He was paranoid we all wanted to steal from him but only thieves steal.

In '73 Monet caused a sensation with a picture of a reclining nude called 'Olympia'. I 'borrowed' from that for one of me own, a parody if you like, 'Study of a Nude: Suzanne Sewing', but I *knew* I was onto something when a critic called Huysmans praised it: "Monsieur Gauguin is the first artist in years to have attempted to represent the woman of today" he wrote.

Glory - marvellous isn't it? It's like booze: a super feeling for a short time and after that it falls, little by little, back into the banal reality. Marvellous praise doesn't pay the rent - it just buys drinks in bars. How long was it, three years? Got a job as a billposter on five francs a day, starved, weight plummeted, shoes and clothes like holes sewn together. But I kept on painting. I always believed my fortune would change and I'd get back with my wife and kids and be a good Dad. Aye and pigs will fly. What a dreamer!

When the 8th Impressionist Exhibition came along I was asked to display something but George Seurat stole the show with 'Sunday Afternoon on the island of Grandes Jatte'- sheer, crazy genius or just plain crazy? Short strokes of pure colour lay side-by-side to leave the eye to mix them. "How did it come about, Georges?" I asked when I met him. "What do you most fear, Gauguin?" he goes, dead posh like. "Most?" I says, "What me Impressionist mates will think of us if I tell them I want to work more in the studio than in the open air." "Then embrace your fear, Paul. Chances are others will fear it too. Fear commands respect. Or they'll laugh. But don't forget: laughter is often an expression of fear." "You sound so . . . well fed, George," I said." "My father indulges me, Paul. Money buys security, security buys time and time buys luxury to experiment. But you'll find neither time nor security in Paris. Try Pont-Aven,

Brittany. I've heard there's an innkeeper who trades paintings for a bed and meals."

Ah, Pont-Aven, Pont-Aven: the Brighton Beach of Brittany and Pension Gloanec run by the able-bodied Madame Gloanec: "A straw mattress and boiled potatoes for one night, Mr Gauguin." she says. I say: "Are you having a laugh, Mrs G?"

"Luckily for you I am, Mr Gauguin," she says.

"You had me going there for a minute, Mrs G! Who else has come to your hotel here in Pont Aven for the summer, Madame?"

"Let me see," she says. "We've a Dutchman: Jacob Meyer De Haan – a most curious specimen if ever I saw one!"

De Haan was *weird!*

"I'm reading zis book, Paul: 'Sartor Resartus' – "Ze Tailor Retailored" in ze English, Thomas Carlyle: "Clozes: zeir origin und influence". It's not about clozes literally of course, clozes are ze metaphor for ze kulture, zrowing off ze old vays und replacing zem wiz new: eine konstant prozess of death und rebirth. You know you really ought to learn ze English. By ze vay, I'm staying at a farm at Le Pouldu, a village a kilometres from here. I've rented a studio. It's private – no tourists. You should come und stay."

And I did and together we got drunk and painted the insides of the kitchen and salon of Hotel Marie-Henry, much to the scandal of the locals.

De Haan reminded me of an intelligent demon. He had a face like a dog's bum with a hat on yes *but* he was as sharp as a razor. In fact, so sharp, I put his ugly mug in some of me work and used some of his ideas almost immediately. 'Symbolism' they called it. Parisian reviewers also happened to champion Symbolism and they recognised their ideas in my new works and gave me good reviews. Of course it was political, but not short sighted - all my work retained this theme: incongruous objects to suggest moods, doubts or alternatives.

"Who else, Madame Gloanec?" I asked her.

"Monsieur Emile Bernard," she says.

"I've heard a rumour that you're claiming to be the inventor of Symbolism in art, Gauguin," goes Emile. "I hope it's not true. You know that it was me who first covered this area. Be warned, Gauguin – history will vindicate me. Meanwhile, I've mail, from another mad Dutchman, like De Haan but not De Haan, Vincent-somebody. Listen to this: 'Gauguin interests me very much as a man, very much. With Gauguin, blood and sex prevail over ambition.' Charming no?"

Very charming – he's honest! Any others, Madame Gloanec?

"Finally, Mr Gauguin, we have also staying with us a Mr Louis Anquetin,"

Ah Louis, Louis, wherefore art thou, Louis? He did 'Avenue de Clichy: Five O'Clock in the evening' - unusual angles, sharp perspectives, cropped figures, ideas lifted from Japanese prints. He lent me a book 'The Marriage of Loti' – a French man in Tahiti – sensational and exciting. Maybe I accidentally mixed it up with stories of my own of sailors abandoned on tropical islands full of naked women, which I suppose is why me, my friend Charlie Laval and thousands of other Frenchmen ended up in Panama in a bold attempt to repeat the Suez success: by linking the Pacific with the Caribbean. It was only 60 kilometres but five hundred thousand million francs and 20,000 dead from malaria? Screw that. We cleared out and went to Martinique, lived in an old hut, ate what we could scavenge and painted the same views, hard to tell one from the other, but I began to feel a style evolving and we returned to Paris in '87, sick as dogs but knowing we'd experienced something that'd affected our work. Unfortunately the Parisian critics didn't share our visions and poor Charlie snuffed it in Egypt soon after from malaria.

And still I starved! But I produced work for the right to starve! Stubborn as sin me!

Science was making rapid progress but the development of aestheticism was slow by comparison - you only had to glance at that shit-heap by Gustave Eiffel in Paris to realise that. Anthropologists had gone to the colonies and taken measurements of bones and catalogued pagan rituals but none had gone to record the beauty of a disappearing Eden. I wanted to but I wasn't quite ready so I went back to Brittany and my second new Dutch friend Vincent Van G went to Arles. Brittany wasn't Tahiti, but better than Paris.

And then, suddenly – wham! I did it. I reached that glorious moment all dedicated artists reach: the moment when all that's clouded and troubled their minds for years drifts away as if by magic and they're blessed, finally, by the beautiful God of Art: I painted 'The Vision After the Sermon'. Mark the tension between the abstract and the natural, the real and the mystical. I *knew* something had happened, felt it, as if a spirit passed into me body, manifested itself through that painting and then left again, moved on to enlighten another. I sacrificed everything – execution, colour and subject – all for *style* and used unnatural colour to express emotion instead of a reflection of the reality I saw.

The civilized world – so-called - is so obsessed with culture, history and traditions and history of cultural traditions, so obsessed with capital, money, celebrity, fame, glamour, glitz and tinsel, it's too easy to forget the chisellers under your nose! The world of art's in the hands of bankers, man. None of the Establishment's education corrupted me but it still gave me an ultimatum: no place at the table until I confessed I was as corrupt as every other fucker. No thanks. I skated free, untarnished. I learnt to paint from real painters, painters who lived by their art and died for their art, not has-beens and nearly-ran's. I painted something out of time for me but they, they looked at their neighbours' face and if he smiled, they smiled too and if they laughed, they laughed also and if they said "This is genius!" they repeated his words.

Vincent and Arles was a marriage of convenience. Theo, his brother, offered to support us both with a little money if we kept on producing (me in Brittany, Vincent in Provence) but ultimately cheaper to have us both under the same roof. Provence won. Anyway, Theo had sold some of me work so I felt obliged.

He paid the rent and there was enough left over to buy important things like tobacco, absinthe and wine – life's essentials. A yellow house! I hated the place and either the wind blew or it rained all the time. Vincent lived like a pig. He couldn't cook. All he did was drink and whore. He really *believed* in a Brotherhood of Art. In his 'brotherhood' I was to be the new 'Messiah', the head of his group. Mad for all that religious shit, the Dutch. I took the piss something chronic and threatened to leave but he went nuts and it came to a head in a square in Arles: he cut off his own fucking ear! I knew then that if I'd stayed he'd have had a go at me so I got the fuck out just before Christmas.

And in that vein, I saw an execution in Paris, January 1890 – Madame La Guillotine. The first attempt was botched - sliced into his face and he lay there in agony drowning in his own blood, begging for death with half a tongue and Death came, straddled the corpse like a triumphant warrior and cast its eyes around for its next victim – me. "How did he die?" that's what they always ask. Not "How did he live?" but always "How did he die?"

When I heard about Vincent's death in July I was sad, not surprised, but sad. After that I had the feeling he was always there, a spirit or a shadow nearby. Not long after I held an exhibition of work from Brittany and Martinique to raise funds and funds raised, I left for the South Seas early April 1891.

Forty-third birthday I sighted Tahiti. I *expected* half-naked tarts with big tits to put flowers in me hair, lead me to a bower of palms and stroke my skin until sunset but *got* a gendarme whose white uniform was too big, harsh colonisation underway with the best land taken, expensive imported foodstuffs, Catholics, Protestants and native beggars with European diseases.

But it wasn't all that bad: first there was Titi, a stupid girl who thought all European men had bottomless pockets and then there was Teha'amana, beautiful Teha'amana with her pocketful of bottom. When not pre-occupied with Teha'amana, I painted fast and furious – the colours, the *colours!* I used yellow for the faces, red for the hair, blue for the clothes, purple for the mountains and an object: a sleeping kitten for peace. When I couldn't afford canvas I used old boards, sackcloth, anything - thirty canvasses and carvings from that first trip then set off back to France and Teha'amana sat at the dockside and watched us go.

"Au revoir, Monsieur Paul! I'll love you always!" she said. I couldn't think of anything except I had enough to shock the world. Not long after, back in Paris, I started coughing blood.

"You've second stage syphilis, Monsieur Gauguin," says the doctor. "You're also suffering from alcohol abuse. I'd estimate that you have perhaps ten years left, though it's hard to say and of course I'm not God." "Thanks for breaking it to us gently,

Doctor" I said with no hint of irony. But God was close wasn't he, finally conferring a blessing upon his disciple? Edgar!

"I've organised your first post-Tahiti exhibition, Gauguin - Paris." He said. "But don't hold your breath – the world isn't yet ready for you but it's a start. Two of them: "Hina Tefatou" and "Te Faaturuma" I'll take for myself. By the way, did you know your Uncle Isidore has died and left you nine thousand francs?"

One door closes and another opens.

"My dear husband," goes the wife, "Please don't squander this inheritance. I ask nothing for myself but consider the children. You may be pleased to know that I'm slowly building up a collection of your work in Copenhagen and an increasing number of students and dealers want to see the pictures. If you don't succeed in Paris, you might always try Copenhagen."

Copenhagen my ass! Instead, I rented a studio in Rue Vercingetorix in Montparnasse. Delius the composer visited, as did Ravel and Grieg and Debussy, a young German artist Munch complimented me on my wooden prints, especially the swirling lines around the figures to emphasise movement, the Swedish writer Strindberg and the sculptor, Rodin. With a wad of cash in me pocket and such illustrious company I was like a dog with two dicks when I met Anna the Javanese wandering lost in the Gare du Lyon. We went to Brittany again in '94, though I should've gone to Copenhagen, and I gave a good account of myself at a fight with some local boys in Concarneau. Have you ever been kicked by wooden clogs? It's special. Fuck civilisation. They can stick it up their ass. That did it for me: back to Tahiti.

How many years did I have left – only nine? I soldiered on in the hope of a miracle. I took a lover: Pau'ura. Within months she was up the duff and I was over the Moon but then one night I heard her voice, under the Moon, beneath the stars: "Mister Paul: the baby we make – she dead."

And *then* a letter from Mette. It never rains but it pours.

"My dear husband, it is with great difficulty and great sadness I must tell you that our daughter Aline has died. She was, as you know, only 19. It happened on New Year's Eve. She went to a Ball with friends. She looked so beautiful in her dress. She returned complaining of a chill and a week later she was gone."

My precious, precious Aline . . .

Then, up the spout again, Pau'ura finally gave me a son and the little Tahitian she taught me came in handy too. 'No te aha oe rir?' translated as 'Why - are - you - angry?' and why was I angry? I was angry because there was life beginning and I had life disintegrating, victim of a terminal disease from the civilized world, the one I'd left behind, the world I was trying to forget but every ache and pain it gave me reminded me it was always going to be there with me until the very end.

So I left Tahiti and went north to the Marquesa Islands with some life left in us but knowing it was a one-way trip, to Hiva Oa and another religious nutcase: Bishop Martin, who reminded me of Bishop Dupanloup. This bastard in a frock owned all the land. It was with great anger I soon realised I was going to have to play politics to get him to give me some to build a house there. So I dressed up and went to see him.

"Monsieur Gauguin," he said grandly, "As you know, since arriving in Hiva Oa from Tahiti all land hereabouts is owned by the Church. To establish a home for yourself the Church would need some evidence that you concurred with its teachings, shall we say? I've noticed since your arrival you've been present at morning Mass almost everyday. I know nothing of your reputation as an artist but I'm impressed with your reputation as a believer. It'll therefore be our pleasure to sell you a piece of land upon which you may build a home."

But guess what? As soon as the ink was dry I'd stop attending the stupid Masses, build my house and find a lover! Oh don't look at me like that - in Polynesia the art of love is as natural as those first walking steps. There are no hypocrites on crucifixes tutting their lips. Don't judge me with your twenty-first century morality. The jungle consumes everything: religion, morality, law, right, wrong, good, bad - all that's drilled into is from birth in the so-called civilized world the jungle consumes as the earth will consume me and you. An abundance of foliage and nature gone mad and we can't help but replicate it. Only when faced with the jungle did I realise just how primitive I truly was. Somebody should tell that to those in Europe for I reckon they've forgotten.

I built up a small collection of flowers: dahlias and nasturtiums. My art dealer in France told me flowers were popular but only French flowers of course. In France they said the native flowers in Polynesia were too fantastic to be true so dahlias and nasturtiums is what they got. And Pastor Vernier befriended me - a Protestant! He kept me supplied with the morphine I needed to cope with the pain as the pox kicked in and my body fell to bits.

"I'm going to get your soul, Gauguin!" Bishop Martin says to us one day, still vengeful.

"But if I take my own life, Bishop Martin, my poor soul will be tainted, dirty, unclean and unfit to enter the spotless kingdom of your God", I says, though it wasn't the first time I'd thought of topping myself. "I doubt you've the courage, Gauguin," he said, and he was right. I was not Vincent."

Vincent came to me often in my dreams.

"How are you, Paul, minen old friend?" he would say in that terrible accent.

"I'm a coward, Vincent!" I would moan.

"Not at all, Paul, not at all! You chose ziss route to buy a few more years unt look at vat you've produced. I, on ze uzzer hand, got ze short straw. I could have done so much more. For ze incident in Arles I apologise, Paul. I was angry you couldn't share mine vision. You know Paul: our influence will filter down through something uz simple uz a drawing zat hangs on ze bedroom wall or ze picture on ze postcard. Now *zat's* revolution. "Ze camera changed everything but you, you knew what had to be done: no longer could ze painter use zee canvas to reflect reality when ze camera did zat much more effectively. We helped re-invent art unt art – like God - brings hope. How do you vant ze vorld to remember you? Show zem how you gave *everything* for vat you believed in. Vat about your "Self-portrait close to Golgotha"? You see? It vas alvays destiny. *You* must end it. And ven you've ended it, you unt I vill sit in ze cafes of Paris like shadows, sip absinthe forever unt watch ze beautiful girls."

Ah, now that's enticing, Vincent, I must admit. See you soon then?

Last Will and Testament of Eugene Henri Paul Gauguin: a dozen carvings, two easels, two palettes, record of military service, cotton trousers and shirts, mosquito net, tobacco and cigarette papers, tinned imported meats, a compass, some wood-working tools, a magnifying glass, a wrench, a green beret, a few bottles of absinthe, ten paintings - my life.

The world makes its artists beg and struggle and then takes their art from them and, with its education, its universities and its big words, it pontificates on 'the nature of genius' over cucumber sandwiches in Sunday afternoon tearooms. Or the world says the artist must suffer on the cross like a reluctant Jesus for the sins of the same world that put the artist there in the first place! And what are the sins? Avarice, envy, fear and stupidity, wrapped up as 'benevolence', 'courage', 'generosity' and 'beauty'.

Each day of my life has been a battle, a battle between the positive and the negative and the strong and the weak. The strong are easy to spot: they speak their minds and make no effort to be everybody's friend. But beware the weak – they are so numerous you can easily be fooled into thinking there's none about! They're those who tell you: you cannot do what they cannot do, coz the weak are more concerned with what others think of them than what they think of themselves.

I spent a few hours listening to my friend the cannibal witch doctor Tioka chanting his mumbo-jumbo about selling immortality in return for surrendering my soul. It wasn't a bad deal and so I signed on the dotted, filled my syringe with a too-large dose of the last of the morphine and wrote a final letter.

"Hiva Oa, April, 1903, to me old friend Charles Morice: Yes, I'm down but not yet defeated. In my opinion, artists have lost all their savagery, all their instinct; one might say their imagination. As a result they act only as undisciplined crowds and feel frightened, lost as it were, when they're alone. Solitude isn't to be recommended to everyone, for you have to be strong in order to bear it and act alone. Thus, I can say: no one taught me anything. On the other hand it's true I know so little, but I prefer that little that's my own creation and, who knows whether that little, when put to use by others, won't become something big?

Within hours I was dead and within half a day six foot under thanks to Martin who smashed what he hated and sold the rest to pay the fine. Oh, did I not tell you about the fine? I'd printed something about the bigots on the island they didn't like. They'd held a trial and found me guilty and I was sentenced to three months in prison and fined. So now you know why Tioka's proposal had such appeal.

At the auction I heard some asshole held one of my Breton snowscape works upside down and sold it as 'Niagara Falls'. Oh, they all had a jolly good laugh. I sat invisible in that courtroom and heard what they would never have dared to say to my face when I was alive. History will judge us and you must judge me.

12 - Leaving Pont-Aven

It was a good show, the best up to that point. It wasn't a chore and it wasn't stressful. I remembered everything and thoroughly enjoyed it and so did my sole audience. But it made no difference to numbers. Maybe I should have stuck it out and written off my loss but at least finished the week's run, maybe. But when you're self-financing everything is a risk and a slip-up is the difference between shopping and leaving with everything you want, or leaving with what you can afford or comes from reduced-to-clear. It's the difference between going out and engaging with the world or spending a week locked in because it's cheaper.

After the show, C and I discussed options and decided to negotiate a withdrawal from Salle Gauguin. I'd had two days of almost zero visitors and every reason to believe I'd have three, four and probably all the same. The end result was it would cost me almost 500€ and no income to balance the outlay. I'd made my point: I'd performed my show at Pont-Aven. Now it was time to see if I could withdraw with some dignity.

That Wednesday night I'd given the Pont-Aven journalist the best performance I'd done and she could have printed a review within two days. Was it too late to make a difference? Maybe not, maybe more would have come Friday and Saturday, but then again maybe they wouldn't. Cancelling three further days might have seemed like a cop-out but it saved 300€ and theatre at my poor end of the scale makes 300 a big number. Otherwise, I had to gamble on whether a coach-load of amateur dramatic enthusiasts, capable of speaking both French and English and with an interest in discovering more about Gauguin, should pass by any time in the next three days and make all the effort financially worthwhile.

On the Thursday, after breakfast, we went to the Town Hall and I explained how things weren't working out and would it be possible to withdraw without it costing too much money. The Secretary looked doubtful and as she went into the Mayor's office to ask him, left the words "It could be you have to pay for all" floating in the air but to his credit Monsieur Le Mayor was generous: provided we left early Friday morning we could have all four days for only one day's rental so I wrote out the balance on the cheque there and then, relieved that it hadn't cost more. Then the phone rang on the Secretary's desk – it was for me. It was a woman in northern Brittany who wanted to come and see the show the following day. The irony was splendid but I apologised but told her we'd had to pull the plug.

From there we parked the car and went out for a walk on foot and up the hill to the Chapel of Tremalo, about two kilometres out of town. Gauguin had visited the squat little stone church a number of times and been inspired by a carved wooden Christ on the cross, that hung high in the rafters near the ceiling. It was this model that was used for his 'Yellow Christ' and from this a number of works on the theme of Christ. He frequently compared himself to the Christ figure, though not necessarily Christ himself, more what Christ represented and endured. A short series of copies were hung in the church along with some explanations. I was struck with 'In the Garden of Olives' when Gauguin saw himself – as Jesus did – abandoned by those close, family and friends, and left to consult his singular fate. I suppose he felt he was making a voluntary sacrifice of all considered normal and respectable at that time, to pursue the lonely life of the painter/artist. C counter-argued he deserved it for abandoning his kids, but his wife had family in Copenhagen so Mette was never completely alone there, as Gauguin was, no family whatsoever, living on a shoestring and getting frequently drunk to block out the highly-volatile reality.

That evening we drove down to Rospico Beach to watch the sunset after an 8.30 show which didn't happen because nobody came. I didn't even bother getting changed. On our return journey from the beach, we got chatting to the local bar owner in an empty bar who told us the whole area round Pont-Aven was like a graveyard after 7 - everybody scurried back home or the GB tourists retreated to the safety of their campsites. But if I'd been told about this some months before it wouldn't have changed my view: I came to Pont-Aven with my art as Gauguin did with his.

Early Friday morning I returned to the Salle, stripped the set and loaded it. Before handing back the keys, P spoke to me one final time: "Jot down 'Gauguin is dead. You won't find his spirit in biscuits, beer, postcards or ice creams. He left Pont-Aven a long time ago and now he is free. Don't look for Nirvana in the footsteps of others' in a felt pen on the back of one of your posters and tape it into the window for the world outside to see before handing back the keys." And I did.

C and I spent two more days in the region: Friday visiting a local abbey, then returned to Le Pouldu to take some contact details, Friday afternoon and Saturday morning on local beaches before driving back to Angers on a blisteringly hot Saturday afternoon.

I'd done it or at least: I'd learned *how* to do it. Eight months planning, writing and re-writing and then adapting it all into French, plus all the rehearsal and scrimping and saving and sacrifice. I'd taken a loss financially but the worst was over and it was on its feet and ready to go out and work its magic. Broken in at Pont-Aven, it will stay in my repertoire for years to come and I hope you get to see it.

I never heard from Gauguin's ghost again. At some time over those last couple of days he must have seen somebody else worth hitching a lift in or on and jumped but I don't know who he chose or when. One minute he was there and the next he was gone.

13 – Adieu, mon ami

I'm blind now.

No, not totally - I see dark and I see light but little between. It's better like this - can't see those scabs . . . it's nearly over, almost. Managed a few bars of Handel's "Messiah" on the old Harmonium, played from memory. Great effort to maintain an even keel, a thread of thought, spasms of pain from arms, legs, and chest and behind the eyes and still the besieged heart patters on.

Here it comes - oh fuck - oh fuck - oh fuck - oh sweet Jesus - oh please, please, please . . . ah, oh . . . oh . . . where are you? Have you abandoned me? It's in vogue these days. Everybody has . . . morphine, syringe, syringe, morphine . . . it's nineteen oh-three now, nineteen oh-three, I made it to the new century, some consolation . . . Tioka came, Tioka . . ." Master," he said, "Master, I can deliver you, Master!" "I'm not a parcel!" I said, grim humour, black humour, savage, primitive Indian humour . . . he chanted, I watched, chanted with candles and incense . . . all the night . . . a spell, a prayer, incantations to the spirits of the dead . . . the morphine, the syringe, the syringe and the morphine . . . Vernier was here, Vernier "The boats can't get through – no more supplies, no more morphine . . . my last bottle Monsieur Gauguin" . . . I can feel the syringe with my fingers, know the operation inside out, could do it blindfolded, ha ha, savage humour, black humour . . . Vincent? Vincent? "Show them how you gave everything for what you believed in, Paul – Self-Portrait Close to Golgotha, it was always destiny" . . . no more boats, no more supplies, the last bottle . . . spirits of the dead watching. . " I can deliver you!" here it comes – oh fuck, oh fuck, oh fuck – oh sweet Jesus spare me – ah, ah, ah, ah . . . oh . . . incantations all through the night, I saw the lights, the spirits of the dead waiting for me, holding out their hands, waiting for me . . . "I can deliver you" . . . It was always destiny, was it always destiny?   . . . I could never have been Jesus, he was too brave . . . he gave but I have it dragged out of me . . . "I can deliver you, Master" How Tioka, how? . . . and then he changed the chant and told me how, and I was mortified, and yet, and yet . . . it would be a final joke on Father Martin . . . the Church wouldn't know . . . what they didn't know wouldn't hurt . . . consecrated ground and yet, and yet . . . I would settle for being a living legend, Father Dupanloup . . . in a few more years my paintings will fetch the price they deserve. A few more years! How will I live to see it? "I can deliver you,

Master, can make you immortal" . . . *Jesus in the desert, forty days and forty nights* . . . *morphine, syringe, syringe, morphine .* . . *no more boats* . . . *good old Tioka, trust Tioka* . . . *here it comes and there it goes* . . . *ah, bliss* . . . *the spirits of the dead are watching* . . . *I pledge my soul to Tioka* . . .

* * *

I died on 8th May 1903 alone in my hut, virtually housebound for almost two weeks, blind and in pain, having suffered two heart attacks.

The last person to see me alive was my neighbour Tioka. Secretly revered as a cannibal witchdoctor, he'd been imprisoned and I'd had his sentence shortened by writing to the judge and as a reward to me Tioka cast a sacred spell and though Martin banned it as heathen he was helpless to stop it. I duped land out of Martin to build my house by pretending to be a churchgoer and as soon as he sold it to me, I stopped going – that made no friends but needs must when the Devil drives eh? Martin was livid. A houseboy Sabu from a local home came in for a couple of hours a day to cook or clean and the only other visitor was Vernier, the Protestant pastor, who acted as the doctor but really wasn't one. It was Vernier who kept me supplied with morphine and in the spring of 1903 a huge sea storm cut off supplies to the island, so Vernier gave me one full bottle and warned I had to make it last but it would probably run out before the next supply. Apart from Vernier, Tioka and Sabu, I saw no one. On May 8th, early in the morning, Tioka went to fetch Vernier. Vernier left soon after but Tioka stayed. He prayed for a while, cross-legged on the floor, burning black animal hair on a tin lid and then appealing to heaven for some response to his words.

"Can you cure my illness and heal my ankle, Tioka?"

He shook his head.

So I said: "How I wish I could live on without pain!" so he leans over and whispered: "Repeat: I pledge my soul to Tioka" and he was serious. I feel a twinge in my chest so I repeated "I pledge my soul to Tioka. I pledge my soul to Tioka. I pledge my soul to Tioka" over and over and a few hours later, around eleven, after the last hypodermic, Sabu runs over to Vernier.

"The Master is dead!"

Tioka sent the boy to Vernier - I saw the boy run through the thick green jungle for five minutes and arrive breathless at the front door of Vernier's house and Vernier answered in his Pastor's outfit. I saw all of this because I was the boy - I was a part of Sabu, he was the first to transport me from my old decayed body to a fresh living body like Vernier and after Vernier to Martin and after Martin to whomever I chose, one by one, like stepping-stones. I hopped on and off and in and out of all of them, learning how to pick and choose and find the right ones to get me to the places I always wanted to go: in the imaginations of other people as no more than a memory or a thought. On the day in question though, Vernier hurried back across to my house but Martin was there first and despite Vernier's pleas for a post-mortem, my body was buried the next day in the Catholic cemetery. Everything he considered sacrilegious was destroyed, including my carved walking stick. But I wreaked a wicked revenge on Martin when I saw him open the back door of the Church one evening at dusk and secretly take his pleasures from one of the local underage girls. I planted the thought "Satan has tempted me and I have fallen into the trap". It was a thought he lived with until his dying day.

My papers were sent back to France and the rest - furniture, pictures, books, my Harmonium, guitar and sculptures were all sold by auction to pay the fine. The auctioneer held one canvas painted in a snowy Brittany upside down and sold it for seven francs as 'Niagara Falls.'

But it didn't matter then and it still doesn't matter now. Now, I drift through your world inspiring those of you who need me, for I was Gauguin and now I am Gauguin's ghost and this was my story.